Step Write Up

JAN COFFEY

Pseudonym for

James A. McGoldrick Ph.D.

Nikoo K. McGoldrick

Copyright © 2009 by Nikoo K. and James A. McGoldrick

All rights reserved. Except for use in any review or face-to-face educational use, the reproduction or utilization of this work in whole or in part in any form by any electronic, mechanical or other means, now known or hereafter invented, including xerography, photocopying and recording, or in any information storage or retrieval system, is forbidden without the written permission of the publisher:

May McGoldrick Books
PO Box 665
Watertown, CT 06795

ISBN: 978-0-9841567-1-9

Printed in the United States of America

CONTENTS

Preface   vii
About the Authors   ix
Introduction   xi

Icebreakers   1
    Icebreaker Questions   3
    Are You an A or a B   5
    Sample Exercise Collection   7

Communication   11
    Puzzle   17
    Triangles   19
    21st Century Skills—Cross-Cultural Communication   21

Collaboration   23
    Fear in a Hat   27
    Photo Scavenger Hunt   28

Creativity   29
    Guided or Free Writing Prompts   33

    Poetry Exercises   35
    Using Imagery   38
    Using Metaphors   40
    Writing Closed Couplets   43
    Writing Open Couplets   45
    Writing Ghazal   47

    Fiction   51
    Using Sense and Imagination   53

    Setting Exercise   55
    Know Your Character   58
    Advance Tips on Character Development   61
    Plot   62
    Plot—Three Act Structure   64
    Plot—the Heroes Journey   66
    The Connection between Character Development and Plot   69
    Point of View   70
    Critiquing   71

Creative Nonfiction   73
    Publishing the Student's Work   78

Articles:
    Write a Nonfiction Book Proposal   79
    Who Am I, and What Am I Missing? Assessing Our Needs as Writers   84
    The Order of Things: Structuring the Synopsis   87
    A Restless Muse   90
    How to Keep Writing While the World Parties Around You   93
    Changing Gears: Writing Suspense vs. Historicals   96
    The A-Z of Rejection   99
    The A-Z of Writing   101

References and Resources   103

Author's Note   105

PREFACE

Step Write Up provides hands-on exercises for teachers in the classroom and for any workshop leader teaching collaboration and writing skills.

This book is the result of creative and collaborative personal and professional endeavors from the two past decades. As a duo of left-brain and right-brain individuals who studied Mechanical Engineering and liberal arts and Sixteenth-Century British Literature, we have always managed to cross the wires in our heads and take a Renaissance approach to life and work.

We've held jobs in submarine construction and as engineering managers for Fortune 500 companies. We've been teachers at the high school and college levels. We've conducted workshops for all age groups on topics of communication, writing, and collaboration. We've collaborated and published twenty-seven works of fiction and one of nonfiction. And we've raised two sons.

So, what have we learned over the years that is worth sharing with you?

We have included exercises on communication and collaboration in this volume that we've used in our classrooms and workshops. You will find lessons on writing poetry and creative nonfiction and fiction.

At the end of this volume, there are a number of articles that we've penned over the years on the topics of writing, publishing, and collaboration. Aside from their usefulness, these are also listed here for your entertainment, as well.

We hope you can put this collection to good use.

ABOUT THE AUTHORS
Jan Coffey

(Pseudonym for Nikoo & James McGoldrick)

Nikoo and Jim McGoldrick are storytellers with a checkered past.

From the submarine shipyards of Electric Boat in Groton, Connecticut, and the clubs of Rodeo Drive, to the forges of Pennsylvania and the electronics manufacturers of Massachusetts, these two have spent their lives gathering material for their novels and their nonfiction.

Professional

- Nikoo is a mechanical engineer and has held jobs in production and as engineering manager.
- Jim, a former college professor, has a PhD in British literature. He currently teaches creative writing and literature at Litchfield High School in Connecticut.

Their Books

- Twenty-seven novels published under three pseudonyms: May McGoldrick, Nicole Cody, and Jan Coffey.
    - MIRA Books. Ten contemporary suspense thrillers under the pseudonym Jan Coffey.
    - Penguin Putnam. Fifteen historical novels under the pseudonyms May McGoldrick and Nicole Cody.
    - Avon/HarperCollins. Two young adult novels.
    - Heinemann. Writing as Nikoo and James A. McGoldrick—one nonfiction work, *A Marriage of Minds*, on collaborative writing.

Awards

- Since 2000, Jim and Nikoo have garnered well over thirty awards for their novels, including the 2009 Connecticut Press Club Best Fiction Award.

The authors reside in Litchfield County, Connecticut.

INTRODUCTION

Twenty-seven published novels, a PhD in literature and a mechanical engineering degree, twenty-five years in high profile management positions, numerous published articles, a wide array of workshops, a how-to book on the craft of collaborative fiction writing, and fourteen years in the classroom at the secondary and post-secondary levels. After all that, the first question people invariably ask when we meet them is, "How *do* you two work together?"

Conditioned (as we all are) by the get-rich-quick, infomercial, sound-bite culture we live in, we know these folks want a one-sentence answer. Here it is:

> Communication + Collaboration + Creativity → Results

Before we started writing together, we spent years in business, training ourselves and working on communication and collaboration skills in such areas as team building, group problem solving, negotiating, and managing…only to suddenly rediscover a quality that we did not even know we had lost. A quality we certainly had in kindergarten. Our creativity. Once that creativity was added to the equation, things began to happen. Successes we'd never imagined began to materialize.

For you and your students, we hope this will be a much easier journey.

On a broader scale, it has taken decades, but the business conglomerates have finally arrived at a consensus that creativity will be a key factor in global survival. From local companies investing in "schools that work" to industry leaders funding foundations, everyone has come to believe that success in the 21st century demands "skills, attitudes, and abilities," in which creativity plays an integral role.

In his recent book, *The Global Achievement Gap*, Tony Wagner identifies what he calls the seven essential "Survival Skills" that our students need in order to compete on a global level:

- critical thinking
- collaborating across networks and leading by influence
- agility and adaptability
- initiative and entrepreneurialism
- effective oral and written communication
- accessing and analyzing information
- curiosity and imagination.

In this book, we attempt to provide exercises that address all of these skills. The section names seem distinct and self-explanatory: Communication, Creativity, and Collaboration. What you will find, however, is that the exercises we have chosen for each section are so interconnected that many of the ones you find in the Communication section could just as easily have been located in the Collaboration section.

You will find that most of the exercises in the Creativity section are aimed at writing fiction, poetry, and nonfiction. That is where our greatest expertise lies.

When we wrote the introduction to our work on collaborative writing, *A Marriage of Minds*, we began with a reference to Edgar Allan Poe's great short story, "The Purloined Letter." In the story, Edgar Allan Poe's sleuth, C. Auguste Dupin, takes on the job of getting back a stolen letter that will surely be used to blackmail a highly placed member of the royal family. To find the letter, he doesn't turn his antagonist's chambers upside down. Unlike his friend, the eminent Prefect of Police, our hero doesn't pry up the floor boards or drill the legs of the chairs in search of hollowed-out hiding places. He doesn't even look behind a single painting.

He doesn't have to.

The object of the Prefect's search, that stolen letter, is right there in the open, tacked to the fireplace mantle where all can see it.

And overlook it.

In a way, teaching students to write creatively can be like that. In kindergarten, all they needed was a sheet of paper and a crayon. One visit to a preschool or a second-grade classroom is all it takes to be reminded of the excitement learning can hold. Ask a child in kindergarten if they can sing or dance or draw a picture or tell a story, and the answer is always yes, yes, yes, and yes. By the time they reach the middle school and high school grades, though, many boys and girls are starting to be convinced that they lack the talent or ability to express themselves creatively. Writing stories and poems is beyond them, they think.

Their English classes have begun to focus on analyzing "classic" literature that many struggle to understand, never mind feel they can emulate. War and abduction and abuse and the Holocaust fill the reading lists. Compared to situations such as these, they think, what experiences have they had that qualify them to write? And as for the type of writing they are doing—creative writing is gone. Expository paragraphs and analytical essays that they will need in college and in business fill the curriculum goals.

So what do we have to offer these youngsters that will rekindle the flame of inspiration in them? What hidden secret do we have that we can share with them to give them back the confidence to write their stories and poems, to develop and apply the creativity needed to meet the challenges of the 21st century? We need to encourage them to "discover."

To accomplish this, we have assembled lessons that can be modified for your own specific personalities, uses, and grade levels. Some are icebreakers that are aimed at promoting communication and collaborative teamwork. Some are lessons that provide for individual creativity and then lead into opportunities for group sharing and (gulp!) critiquing. And we go even further, showing how the products of these creative efforts can even carry us into areas of initiative and entrepreneurialism.

There is a short "lead-in" to many of the lessons. In each of those, we refer to New York State Curriculum Standards that the content of the lesson addresses.

We hope this book can help students grow through the experience of these exercises. Later on, when they are adults and looking for that satisfying feeling that comes with creating something special—whether it is done individually or collaboratively, in their garret in Brooklyn or in their shared cubicle in Albany—they'll know where to find it. Like that letter in Poe's story, it will be right out in the open.

And they'll see it.

ICEBREAKERS

Musicians know they have to *tune* their instruments before playing a song. Teachers and instructors recognize that they have to persuade their audience to *focus* in order to have a successful class.

Icebreakers are a key to helping students become attuned with the environment of the class and to release tension. Icebreaker games help to create a positive group atmosphere. They encourage the participants to relax and to break down social barriers and to interact. The individual activities are great tools for the instructor to use for energizing and motivating the class. They help the group dynamics by teaching team-building while encouraging each individual to "think outside the box."

Icebreaker games, also known as motivators and team builders, are used in preschool environments and in corporate boardrooms and in social situations. There are hundreds of well-known tested games and dozens of variations of each used every day. In the following few pages, we've included instructions for several icebreaker activities. Please use any variation of them as you see fit in your own classrooms. Also, at the resource section of this book, we've listed a dozen websites where you can find similar types of activities.

New York State Standard 4.1 Language for Social Interaction

Oral communication in formal and informal settings requires the ability to talk with people of different ages, genders, and cultures, to adapt presentations to different audiences, and to reflect on how talk varies in different situations.

Students (Intermediate):
➢ *use verbal and nonverbal skills to improve communication with others.*

This is evident, for example, when students:
➢ *participate in small group discussions in class*

EXERCISE — Icebreaker Questions

A great way to help students open up and participate in the class is to ask them leading questions that allow them to express their personality or share interesting things about themselves. The same question can be asked of students across the room, and an occasional 'why' here and there after the answer will encourage more discussion. The idea is to get everyone involved.

Here is a list of twenty safe, useful icebreaker questions to help break the ice:

1. Are you a morning or night person?
2. If I could be anybody besides myself, I would be…
3. What's your favorite cartoon character? Why?
4. What's the movie you've seen ten times?
5. What's the movie you've seen twenty times? Has anyone seen a movie twenty times?
6. If you were an animal, what would you be?
7. If you could have an endless supply of any food, what would you get?
8. What's your least favorite food?
9. What's the weirdest thing you've ever eaten?
10. If you were an ice cream flavor, which one would you be and why?
11. When you were little, who was your favorite super-hero and why?
12. What is one goal you'd like to accomplish during your lifetime?
13. If they made a movie of your life, what would it be about and which actor would you want to play you?
14. What's the ideal dream job for you?
15. Who is your hero? (a parent, a celebrity, an influential person in one's life)
16. Name one of your favorite things about someone in your family.
17. If you could visit any place in the world, where would you choose to go and why?
18. What's your favorite thing to do in the summer?
19. What are your favorite hobbies?
20. If you had to describe yourself using three words, they would be…

And some extras:

1. What are your pet peeves?
2. What is one interesting thing about you that *you* dislike?
3. Tell us about a unique or quirky habit of yours.
4. If someone made a movie of your life, would it be a drama, a comedy, a romantic-comedy, an action film, or science fiction?
5. The hands of the world's clocks are going to freeze on a certain day of the week and time. What's your choice?
6. What will you be doing five years from now?

Note: These same questions can be used as writing prompts for students who do daily guided free writing in a journal.

EXERCISE—Icebreaker

Are you an A or a B

Purpose

This fast-paced exercise helps students to understand each other better and also appreciate their differences as well as commonalities. It generates lots of movement and laughter, so it is a good choice as an icebreaker.

What You Need

- Two signs to hang on the walls in two sides of the class room. The signs should read "A" and "B"
- Papers
- Pens
- Tape

Preparation

- Prepare the class room by placing sign "A" on one side of the room and sign "B" on the other side of the room. You may put a tape on the floor to divide the area.
- Make sure students can freely move between the two signs, with chairs or tables or desks moved safely out of the way.

Setup

To keep this exercise entertaining and educational, keep the pace moving steadily.

- Ask all the students to come to the center of the room.
- Explain that you are going to read through a number of pairs of statements. Those who feel that they are similar to the first concept in each pair, should move near to sign 'A' and those that feel closer to the second concept, should move to sign 'B.'

> Explain that you will read the series of pairs one after another. Students should continuously respond by moving to different points in the room depending on their preference.

Here are some ideas for the list. You should customize this list based on your own needs:

Okay. Are you ready? Here we go. Are you ___ or ___?

> - Day…Night
> - A Pen…A Pencil
> - Dark chocolate…Milk chocolate
> - The Sun…The Moon
> - Hot…Cool
> - Yes…No
> - Summer…Winter
> - 1…2
> - An only child…Not
> - Sweet…Sour
> - Red…Blue
> - A dog…A cat
> - Eat Fast Food…Eat Healthy
> - Blonde…Brunette

Add to these. The questions can be more personal, depending on the issues you'd like to address with regards to the students' background or outside school environment or even underlying problem issues the group might have.

Ask the students if they could spot patterns and if they thought some of their classmates were on "their side" more often than others.

EXERCISE—Icebreaker Sample Collection

Catch Ball

This is a great exercise to use for introductions or for reinforcing concepts or to have student's attention on the instructor as the ball could be tossed to any individual in the classroom to answer a question.

Toss a ball to one of the students, who then introduces himself or herself. This student then throws the ball to someone else. Challenge the class to complete the introductions without the ball being dropped.

The same exercise can be used by asking the question as you toss a ball to the student. The idea is to distract the student's conscious attention so that the answer can surface from the subconscious.

Candy

Have a bag of M&M or other small candies to pass around. Each person must tell one thing about himself or herself for each piece of candy taken.

"Do-It-Yourself" Nametags

Have everyone create nametags with drawing or stickers representing their activities and interests. Have each person introduce themselves and explain the items on their nametags.

EXERCISE—Icebreaker Sample Collection (continued)

Change...

This simple exercise makes people aware of the impact of change.

Ask the students to fold their arms. Then ask them to fold their arms the other way around. Wait in silence for a few moments before asking them to unfold their arms.
Ask questions: How difficult it was to fold their arms the other way? Who had difficulty? Who didn't? Encourage discussion.

Rebel Foot

This is a good exercise for self-awareness and releasing tension.

Make sure that the students are sitting comfortably. Now ask them to lift their right foot off the floor and make clockwise circles and, while doing this, ask them to draw the number '6' in the air with their right hand.
Their feet will change direction, and there's nothing they can do about it!

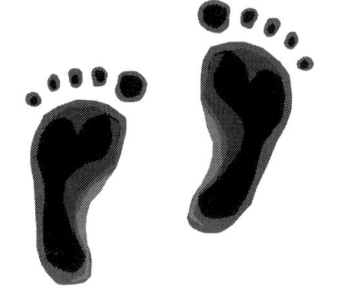

Decision Making

This exercise is good for teamwork and decision-making principles.

Divide the students into groups of 4–6. Give them a map or a road atlas and ask them to decide what the best route is between two points.

Ask them what process they used to reach agreement and arrive at a decision. Encourage thinking outside of the box. Perhaps someone drove to the nearest airport and flew to the destination. There are no wrong answers.

EXERCISE—Icebreaker Sample Collection (continued)

Uses for a...

This is the classic brainstorming exercise where the class is presented with an object - such as a pen or a plastic cup, or a bag - and the group is challenged to write down as many uses as they can think of for the object.

Toss the catch ball around and encourage students to share one answer at a time.

Mind Reader

Ask everyone in the group to:

- Pick a whole number between 1 and 10 and keep it secret.
- Multiply this number by 9.
- If this number has 2 digits, add them together.
- Subtract 5 from this number.
- Correspond this number to a letter of the alphabet (1 = A, 2 = B, 3 = C etc).
- Think of a country that starts with that letter.
- Think of an animal beginning with the second letter of that country.

Then ask "How many people were thinking of an elephant in Denmark?"

EXERCISE — Icebreaker Sample Collection (continued)

Surgeon's Dilemma

Unfortunately, stereotypical thinking is part of our everyday lives and one of the major barriers to awareness. Generalizations can help to make sense of the world but they can also seriously mislead us. Here's an old one that still catches the students:

A young man who had been injured in a car accident is taken to the emergency room. The doctor in charge determines that emergency brain surgery is required. Immediately, the brain surgeon is paged. Upon seeing the patient, the surgeon exclaims, 'Oh no, I can't operate on that boy! He's my son!'

The surgeon is <u>not</u> the boy's father. Explain this.

The answer:
The surgeon is the boy's mother.

Crime Scene

A good exercise for developing creative thinking, logic, and questioning techniques. Pose this scenario to the group:

A man — Pip — was found hanging by the neck from a single beam in his room. Otherwise, the room was completely empty. The only door was locked and bolted with the key still in the lock on the inside of the door. The only window was closed with the security bolts in place. There were no signs of a forced entry. Time of death was estimated to have been 8 hours ago. There was a damp patch on the floor which later proved to be water — not blood. How did Pip die?

Encourage students to ask questions, but only give 'Yes' or 'No' answers.

Crime Scene Solution
Pip committed suicide. He dragged a block of ice into the room, stood on it, tied the rope around his neck and waited for the ice to melt...

COMMUNICATION

Communication:

> A process by which information is exchanged between individuals through a common system of symbols, signs, or behavior.
> —*Merriam Webster*

> Two-way process of reaching mutual understanding, in which participants not only exchange (encode-decode) information but also create and share meaning.
> —*Business Dictionary*

Researchers, academics, the business community…everyone agrees that communication skills are essential for success in today's knowledge-based society. But effective communication is rarely taught and even more rarely learned in our society.

Partnership for 21st Century Skills specifically identifies "communicate clearly" as a goal for every student, and the student needs to be able to:

- Articulate thoughts and ideas effectively using oral, written, and nonverbal communication skills in variety of forms and contexts.
- Listen effectively to decipher meaning, including knowledge, values, attitudes, and intentions
- Use communication for a range of purposes (e.g. to inform, instruct, motivate, and persuade.

Easily said, but difficult to accomplish.

Communicating clearly involves using multiple channels that we humans have developed over the centuries. Some of them are primal in nature, like body language, and some are acquired over years, like the tone of one's voice, the attitudes, language, personality types, cultural diversity, emotions, perspectives, up-bringing, and intentions. Communication is far more complex than most of us even think about.

In our own situation as collaborative writers, communicating effectively with each other has been the foundation upon which our collaboration is based on. But we didn't build this house overnight. Despite years of management and communication training and a great marriage to start with, the process was excruciatingly slow and took years to accomplish. And why was that?

> "We only hear half of what is said to us, understand only half of that, believe only half of that, and remember only half of it."
> --*University of Maine Effective Communication Bulletin #6103*

Ferdinand Fournies, an expert on management in the workplace, explains the phenomenon in this way:

> The mind thinks at least six times faster than we can speak, and because the mind thinks so much faster, its primary function is a *reactive function*. Of course, the mind receives the information transmitted, but the information is received so fast that the mind reacts even before the message is completed.

As a part of an exercise that we've included in this section ("Puzzles"), we have two participants sit with their backs to each other. While one tries to describe a geometric pattern, the other—in almost every case—cannot wait for the complete set of instructions and races ahead, speculating on what the outcome will be and then trying to see if the instructions that follow support their assumptions.

This is natural. After all, we are all creative thinkers, and we cannot put our creativity on hold. When a partner begins to explain a shape, an image, or a character, the listener cannot tell his or her imagination to wait. No, the predictions that the listener makes about the image are limited only by the parameters that the speaker creates. It is only through the give-and-take of questions and answers that the image becomes more and more ordered. More coherent.

It is through clear communication that the image subtly evolves, eventually becoming the creation of both speaker and listener.

There are two basic rules that we always try to keep in mind in communication. These are the cement and forms that create a building's foundation.

- ➢ Organize thoughts in your mind before sharing them with others.
- ➢ Communication is collaborative, not *competitive*.

Communicating effectively helps members of a group build trust and respect, fostering learning and allowing the group to accomplish their goals.

When asked to define communication, most people refer to the techniques used to express their wants, namely talking. But in a team environment, listening is the key.

To improve communication, active listening should be part of the group's culture. Stressing the word 'active' with regard to listening, we want to share a few hints about how to achieve a winning method of communication.

- ➢ Make certain the atmosphere surrounding you and the group is informal and relaxed. Minimize distractions.
- ➢ Repeat what the speaker says. Not word for word. Just the gist of it. A paraphrase of it. This helps the discussion remain focused and on track, and sends a signal back that what was just said actually registered.
- ➢ Ask relevant, open-ended questions, beginning with "What…How…or Please explain."
- ➢ Summarize and clarify.
- ➢ Give an opinion if the speaker is willing to hear your opinion.

The other half of communication is speaking and expressing what you think. This should be done in clear and non-defensive way. Individuals communicate as much or more through body language as they do with words. Body language includes facial expressions, eye contact, and stance or movement of arms and hands.

Examples of body language that support effective communication include an open body stance, sitting on the edge of your chair, and maintaining eye-contact. Crossing your arms, pointing fingers, and casting side glances serve to block communication.

When working in any group, there are bound to be moments of conflict and anger. Here are guidelines to have in place when we are angry:

- Use "I" statements. This avoids making the listener defensive. Let the group know why you are upset.
- Avoid judgments. Don't exaggerate.
- Show interest in the ideas and feelings of other people in the group, too. This tends to relax the situation.
- Get agreement regarding what the issue is.
- Invite the group to join you in addressing the issue.
- If the group is not responsive, take a break and come back to it at a different time. We call this 'sleeping on it.' Sometimes an issue that we were ready to go to battle about is a non-issue the next day or next week.

Dialogue is one important part of communication. We like to compare it to practicing a sport. You build skills as you work at it. Yes, speech classes work, but not all of us have the time or money to enroll in one of those. Here is a listing of important dialogue skills:

- Allow others to finish speaking.
- Respect others' thoughts, feelings, views, even when they differ from your own.
- Listen actively without distracting.

Don't forget that no matter how brilliant your idea, it is worthless unless you can share it with others. Effective communication is crucial at every stage of life.

New York State Standard 1 Language for Information and Understanding

1.1 Listening and reading to acquire information and understanding involves collecting data, facts, and ideas; discovering relationships, concepts, and generalizations; and using knowledge from oral, written, and electronic sources.

Students (Intermediate):
- *interpret and analyze information from…reference materials, audio and media presentations, oral interviews…electronic data bases intended for a general audience*
- *compare and synthesize information from different sources*
- *use a wide variety of strategies for selecting, organizing, and categorizing information*
- *distinguish between relevant and irrelevant information, and between fact and opinion*
- *relate new information to prior knowledge and experience*
- *understand and use the text features that make information accessible and usable, such as format, sequence, level of diction, and relevance of details.*

Students (Commencement)
- *synthesize information from diverse sources and identify complexities and discrepancies in the information*
- *make distinctions about the relative value and significance of specific data, facts, and ideas*
- *make perceptive and well developed connections to prior knowledge*

1.2 Speaking and writing to acquire and transmit information requires asking probing and clarifying questions, interpreting information in one's own words, applying information from one context to another, and presenting the information and interpretation clearly, concisely, and comprehensibly.

Students (Intermediate):
- *organize information according to an identifiable structure*
- *develop information with appropriate supporting material, such as facts, details, illustrative examples or anecdotes, and exclude extraneous material*

New York State Standard 4 Language for Social Interaction

1. Oral communication in formal and informal settings requires the ability to talk with people of different ages, genders, and cultures, to adapt presentations to different audiences, and to reflect on how talk varies in different situations.

Students (Intermediate):
- ➤ *express ideas and concerns clearly and respectfully in conversations and group discussions*
- ➤ *learn some words and expressions in another language to communicate with a peer or adult who speaks that language*
- ➤ *use verbal and nonverbal skills to improve communication with others.*

Students (Commencement):
- ➤ *engage in conversations and discussions on academic, technical, and community subjects, anticipating listeners' needs and skillfully addressing them*

Communication Exercise—Puzzle

To prepare for this lesson, cut five identical squares out of paper or cardboard for one participant. Copy the diagram (found in the next page) as a handout for the second participant (the director.)

Sit one student (the director) in a chair with his or her back to a partner (the arranger) or to any number of arrangers who are sitting on the floor or at a table.

The director's task is to look at the diagram and give clear directions to the arrangers in how they are to position their squares. The director cannot look at the arrangers' work. The director should start with the top square and describe each one in succession. The director should pay close attention to the relationship of each square to the one before and after it. NO QUESTIONS from the arrangers.

After a period of five minutes, if the exact image is not assembled, allow questions and answers.

Note: If multiple arrangers are working simultaneously, it will be difficult to have them work independently…but that may provide some unexpected results, too! Still, encourage independent work.

This exercise can be a competition, too, with points awarded to the best director. Just sketch out different arrangements of the squares for different directors.

Communication Exercise—Puzzle

Instructions: Study the series of squares below. With your back to the group, you are to direct the participants how they are to arrange the figure. Begin with the top square.

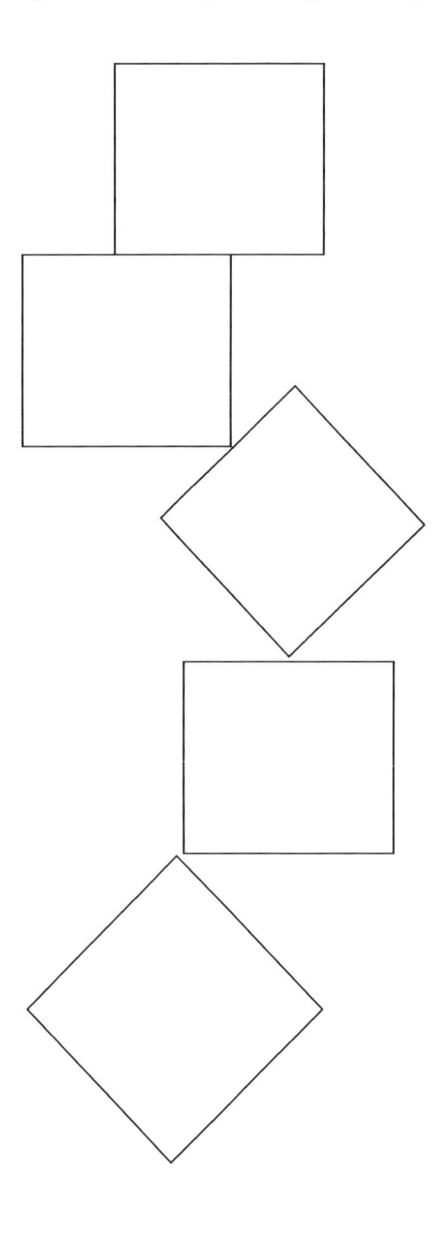

Communication Exercise
Diagram 1

Communication Exercise—Triangles

Who Draws the Most Triangles?

This is an excellent team-building and communication exercise. Divide the audience into groups of three people per team.

➢ Part 1

Pass out three pens to each team (three different color pens, if possible) and a clean sheet of paper.

The object of the game is to draw as many triangles as time permits, but each person is only allowed to draw one leg of each triangle.

Group members cannot speak before or during the exercise.

Start the timer for 45 seconds. Groups start drawing triangles.

Stop time. Groups count and report how many triangles they were able to draw.

The instructor will record the results.

➢ Part 2

Pass out clean sheet of paper.

Each team takes 1 minute and brainstorms a strategy within their group.

The object of the game is to draw as many triangles as time permits, but each person is only allowed to draw one leg of each triangle.

Groups can speak during the exercise.

Start the timer for 45 seconds. Groups start drawing triangles.

Stop time. Groups count and report how many triangles they were able to draw.

The instructor will record the results.

➢ Part 3

Pass out clean sheet of paper.

Each team takes 4 minutes and brainstorms a strategy within their groups.

The object of the game is to draw as many triangles as time permits, but each person is only allowed to draw one leg of each triangle.

Groups can speak during the exercise.

Start the timer for 45 seconds. Groups start drawing triangles.

Stop time. Groups count and report how many triangles they were able to draw.

The instructor will record the results.

The result: Everyone plays a part in the success of the team. Productivity increases with good communication. Have an open discussion comparing the results.

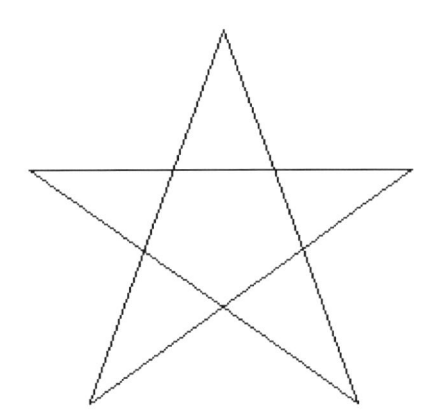

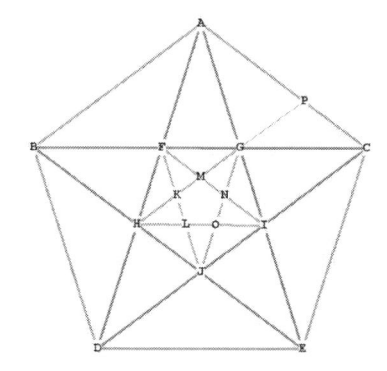

21st Century Skills—Cross-cultural communication

Global communication and awareness is an important part of the 21st century skills we need to be developing. Short of learning a foreign language in its entirety, there are actions that can be taken in the classroom to heighten our global awareness and improve our cultural 'competence.

Set aside time at the beginning of each class on a regular basis for a "culture moment." These don't have to be deep and heavy; they are intended to be team builders as well as cultural learning opportunities. From the examples listed below, consider using one or two for projects that can be presented by the class to younger groups.

Examples:

- Learn and share a great expression in a less frequently taught foreign language such as Arabic, Chinese, Hindi, Japanese, Korean, Farsi, or Turkish.
- Try out an ethnic food recipe and bring in a sample for everyone (after finding out about allergies…).
- Have students research an action that we do in our everyday lives that is not appropriate in another culture (i.e. wearing shoes in the house in a Muslim or Japanese household).
- Listen to a current popular song from another culture (they are on the Internet).
- Watch few moments of a movie in different culture and language.
- Have the group research a national or cultural holiday and celebrate it.
- Challenge the class to research and come back with as many different languages for "thank you" as possible. Afterward, share with them that there are approximately 2800 languages and dialects, and 6 billion people in the world.
- The cultural history of a student's name or some unusual name in their family is always interesting research. (We did this and a student was stunned to find out that his great, great grandfather had been in charge of the Spanish navy in Cuba during the Spanish-American War.)
- Have groups of students work on a current topic from the United Nations website (www.un.org) and share it with the class.

COLLABORATION

Framework documents for 21st century skills include numerous references to teamwork and collaboration.

- ➤ Work Creatively with Others
    - o Develop, implement and communicate new ideas to others effectively
    - o Be open and responsive to new and diverse perspectives; incorporate group input and feedback into the work

- ➤ Collaborate with Others
    - o Demonstrate the ability to work effectively and respectfully with diverse teams
    - o Exercise flexibility and willingness to be helpful in making necessary compromises to accomplish a common goal
    - o Assume shared responsibility for collaborative work, and value the individual contributions made by each team member

- ➤ Work Effectively in Diverse Teams
    - o Respect cultural differences and work effectively with people from a range of social and cultural backgrounds
    - o Respond open-mindedly to different ideas and values
    - o Leverage social and cultural differences to create new ideas and increase both innovation and quality of work

And what do we have to say about this topic after spending nearly two decades of collaborating in life as well as literature?

- ➤ **Harness the creative synergy.**

Synergy is a 17th-century word that has been dominating the business world for the past three decades. Pure and simple, synergy means the power of cooperative effort.

If you plant certain plants close together, the roots commingle and actually improve the quality of the soil, so that both plants will grow better than if they were grown separately.
If you put two pieces of wood together—as in the laminating process—they will hold much more than the weight each could hold separately.

The principle behind synergy is that the whole is greater than the sum of its parts. One plus one equals three...or more.

Nikoo's engineering-trained left brain might disagree with the last statement, but her right brain accepts it completely.

> Clapping with the right hand only produces no noise. –Malay Proverb

> When spider webs unite, they can tether a lion. –Ethiopian Proverb

> Two heads are better than one. –Circus Sideshow Proverb

In collaborative writing, we have a partner who brings to the work another point of view and a different command of the language. They bring an additional world of experiences. They can encourage us and help us through difficult scenes. The same principals apply to learning and innovation skills. These same basic concepts are essential in everyday life in dealing with partners or with our children. These same ideas are used in successful businesses around the world.

Before moving on to the exercise section on this topic, it is only right to mention that collaboration naturally entails a certain level of stress and disagreement. But there are steps one can take to make the road much easier to travel. Here are some of the adjustments that we had to make *consciously* to enhance our collaboration experience. These same ideas can be stressed with students.

➢ Respect…respect…respect…for your team members. The words are self-explanatory.

- Lose the focus on *I*! Refocus on *WE*! It is important to shed the 'me' mentality and learn the meaning of 'us.' This is not *my* work, *my* idea, *my* individual effort; this is *our* work, *our* idea, *our* combined effort! We've all seen that poster, "There's no 'I' in TEAM." Clichéd as it is, it's worth saying again.

- Resign the charter membership to "Annoyances, Inc." The constant tapping of the pen on the table. The unsuccessful stifling of a yawn. The negative shaking of the head during a brainstorming session. Not listening. You can think of dozens of scenarios when disruptions can occur. Now would be an excellent time to go back and read the section on communication again.

- If there is one thing we've learned to keep in mind during all the years of working together, it is that collaboration is a process of continual change. No two days are necessarily the same. No two books are written in the exact same order. The process changes. Flexibility and the willingness to make compromises are very important. The team's common goal is the single thing that needs to be kept in mind.

- For us, it helps to maintain a sense of humor when it comes to disagreements. Nothing is blown out of proportion…if we can help it. We like to communicate (and protect our relationship) through humor. From experience we know that, like a virus, a sour mood can be contagious, damaging, and counterproductive in the work environment. We are always ready to laugh at our own failings.

- Make sure everyone on the team understands the common goal.

- Establish routine. Sometimes routines need to be revised. As we mentioned above, flexibility and compromise are part of the collaboration process. Still, routine gives us the framework to complete a project in a timely fashion.

We'd like to share with you a statement we used to sell a book on collaboration a few years ago to Heinemann Publishing. Here it is…we still believe it.

Collaboration enhances creativity! How else would the human race continue to propagate itself? Why, even Dolly the sheep (of the Clan MacClone) was the product of collaborative scientific effort! The same holds for life....

New York State Standard 4   Language for Social Interaction

4.1. Oral communication in formal and informal settings requires the ability to talk with people of different ages, genders, and cultures, to adapt presentations to different audiences, and to reflect on how talk varies in different situations.

Students (Intermediate):
- listen attentively to others and build on others' ideas in conversations with peers and adults
- express ideas and concerns clearly and respectfully in conversations and group discussions
- use verbal and nonverbal skills to improve communication with others.

Students (Commencement):
- engage in conversations and discussions on academic, technical, and community subjects, anticipating listeners' needs and skillfully addressing them
- express their thoughts and views clearly with attention to the perspectives and voiced concerns of the others in the conversation

Collaboration Exercise—Fear in a Hat

This teambuilding and cohesion activity is suitable for the beginning of a term or a program.

Each student anonymously writes down his or her personal fears or worries on a sheet of paper which are then collected in a hat and read aloud. This leads to a good discussion centered on possible shared fears.

Materials:
- Writing utensils
- Small slips of paper
- Hat (or box)

Setup:
Distribute the paper and allow about five minutes of writing time. Instruct the students to write anonymously, but to be as specific and honest as possible about a fear or worry they have. They can write more than one, but each fear/worry should be on a separate slip of paper. Collect the papers.

Shuffle the slips and ask one person to take a 'fear' out of the hat and read it aloud to the rest of the class. The reader should attempt to explain and elaborate on what the person who wrote the fear might have meant. Have everyone simply listen…and then go on to the next reader.

After all fears have been read and elaborated on, discuss as a class what some of the common fears were or what connections they see between the fears and worries.

This activity can help build trust and unity, as students realize that many of them have similar fears.

This exercise is suitable for all group sizes.

You can also try a variation of Happiness in a Hat…but anticipate VERY different results!

Collaboration Exercise—Photo Scavenger Hunt

Photo Scavenger Hunt is a collaboration-based scavenger hunt that can be conducted over the period of two or more classroom periods.

The goal is to bring back digital photos of places and things, printing them out and arranging the photos in the classroom as a collage. Groups make presentations to an audience at the end of the project.

This is an active teambuilding activity. The recommended group size is three or four students. You will need a digital camera (or cell phone) for each team.

Setup:
As a class, prepare a list of about twelve interesting places, things, and circumstances that can be captured, using a camera. Some examples are:

- Friends
- A family of animals
- Wind
- A very relaxing place
- Knowledge
- Something big and the color red
- Funny
- The smallest tree
- Traffic
- A group photo with someone dressed in very formal attire
- Happy
- Hair

Encourage creativity with this list. Make them think. There are no right or wrong answers to anything (only appropriate and inappropriate). The class must decide what each image should be. Make enough copies of the final list for each team.

Playing the Photo Scavenger Hunt
Divide the group into teams of about three to four people. Distribute cameras and copies of the list you made. Explain the rules of the activity. Set a time limit for the groups (Limiting time helps the collaboration process). Instruct the teams to find as many things as they can on the list in the designated time. Encourage the players to be creative and to think outside the box.

The printed pictures should be trimmed and arranged in a collage on a poster board, and each group should present their project for display and/or group discussion.

CREATIVITY

At one time or other in our lives, we have all had within us a creative voice crying out to be discovered.

Nikoo

I had just turned twelve when the tragedy occurred. My classmate, my confidante, my best friend died in a hit-and-run accident one afternoon. All she did was chase a ball into the street. Torn between the anguish of the loss and the need to express my grief somehow, I turned to writing. I sat down and drafted a short story. I poured my heart and soul into those words.

The story dealt with an orphan boy, about my age, who is given a caged bird as a gift by a stranger on a bus. Bringing the gift home, he is faced with the anger of a jealous older sister who complains that she will end up having to take care of the creature. During the verbal argument that follows, the bird escapes the cage. The boy, chasing after it, is hit by a car and dies.

Sad? I thought it was! But to my adolescent mind, the story was filled with all kinds of images of kindness and generosity and freedom that I thought were important facets of how we view and deal with life...and death.

I read my work in my literature class at school, and the story was met with great enthusiasm by my classmates. Full of myself, I brought the work home and read it to my mother.

Her reaction was a bit different. She took me to counseling.

Hurt may not be the best word to describe my feelings at the time. I did, however, lose enthusiasm for an audience.

It was then that I started a diary that turned to a regular journal of ideas, feelings, and even stories. My writing became something very private, in spite of the growing volume of work. I valued the satisfaction that the written words gave me, but at the same time I cared very little about polish or perfection. After all, this was all for my eyes only.

I guess this is still my style. I always have ideas floating in my head, and I have the ability to put them down on the paper at a pretty good rate. Now, as far as revision and fine-tuning and finish, well...

Jim

One late summer night, my older brother (who was probably around eleven years old, at the time) entertained the entire family with a poem he'd written about his throne and his throne room. The "throne" room was tiled, with a big mirror, and a tub. I must have been going into second grade, and I remember lying in bed and listening to the laughter floating up the stairs.

Wow! They were really having fun, and I wanted to be a part of it. So I decided that I'd write a poem, too. But what could I write about?

I remember looking out the window into the dusk at the utility poles on the street. They looked like crosses.

So I wrote my poem. Serious and religious as only a seven-year-old can write serious and religious. Did I mention that it was serious?

The response was....well, polite. Very nice, they said, stealing looks at one another.

Time for bed!

Although I was disappointed with the response, I continued to write poems. Most of the time, though, I wrote just for myself.

I like poetry. I like the conciseness. I like the impact. I like the finish.

All these years later, that's still my style, I suppose. I like coming up with stories and characters, but even more, I like the feel of language. I like imagery that conveys meaning. I like structure. I like revising work to look stylish, finished.

Creative opportunities liberate one's mind to cross into personal zones of higher thinking. These traits and habits stay with us in life, sometimes in our active everyday lives, and other times in the form of a soft murmur in the background.

Dr. Howard Gardner's book *Creating Minds* and Dr. Mel Levine's *A Mind at a Time* list certain behavioral patterns that come with creativity. These traits promote originality; they are the traits of the artist:

- **Divergent Thinking**. Allowing your mind to go off on tangents.
- **Top Down Processing**. Being highly subjective in reacting to information and experience. Intermingling your own values and perspective over much of what you come across. The creative machinery can't stop and will improve assignments.
- **Return to Naiveté**. Assuming a new point of view.
- **Risk Taking**. We resign ourselves to being controversial. It's okay being wrong sometimes.
- **The Integration of Technical Skill with Originality**. There's always room for innovative thinking. Steve Jobs (Apple CEO) told the following story at Stanford's graduation. He said, "You know, I dropped out of Reed College and had nothing to do, so I took a course in calligraphy. And it all went into the Mac keyboard!" That was a question of style and it helped to define Apple's niche.
- **Autonomy from Peer Pressure and Standards**. This is a very difficult issue, especially in teen years. Many young people are so focused on pleasing their friends that they forego their own creativity. There are no easy steps to take to overcome this, but it is an issue that deserves attention by parents and educators.
- **Suspension of Self-Evaluation**. Regardless of age, we are all guilty of not being able to shut down the critic inside of us. Julia Cameron spends a great deal of her book *The Artist's Way* suggesting a spiritual path that will help overcome the inner critic and find a way to greater creativity.
- **Discovery and Pursuit of the Right Medium**. The search for the 'right' channel for our creative drive was an easy one for us. We both wanted to be writers as long as we could remember. Our sons, on the other hand, have never limited themselves to one medium. They are writers, musicians, actors. There's no reason to decide on one so long as you are pursuing the creativity.
- **Stylistic Distinctiveness**. To develop a unique voice is a lifetime of work that starts at a young age. Great artists become distinctive rather than imitative.

As you can tell by now, we are believers in the importance of creativity as a way of life. But before we move on to specific creative writing exercises, we want to share a passage we came across from one of the country's top learning experts.

> Opportunities to be creative and to brainstorm can be the salvation of children who are having a hard time succeeding academically. Art classes, music classes, and creative writing opportunities should be considered core curriculum in a nation that values and harbors a tradition of innovation. Some kids were born to create better than they learn. For them, in particular, the discovery of the right medium, the acquisition of technical skill, and the finding of a nurturing environment within which to try some creative leaps all boost self-esteem and motivation. (Levine 213)

The specifics or the ingredients, as we like to call them in some of the workshops we conduct on creative writing, are these:

- Expertise. Don't be afraid. Experts were not born experts. They garnered skills through practice. And this is an area where we can help. In the areas of poetry, fiction, and creative nonfiction, we've provided exercises that help acquire skills that lead to expertise.

- Talent. We mention it, but we have little to say about it. Without the next ingredient, so much promising talent will simply languish. At the same time, many writers with average or below average talent succeed because of…

- Hard work. Passion. Tenacity. Motivation and drive. We like to compare creativity and writing to exercise regimens. This week, you run or walk ten minutes a day. Next week, you go twenty minutes a day. The process is an easy one that you can continue to build on, conditioning yourself, extending your endurance. Soon you're successfully running marathons. Writing is the same. Fifteen minutes a day…or one page. Next week, thirty minutes a day…or three pages. You see where this is going. But…if you stop and do it only occasionally, you never reach your top condition. Steven King says he writes 365 days a year. Our own goal is to maintain that same level of commitment. We've realized that ideas and words come to us so much easier when we stay in the habit of writing every day.

This is where Thomas Friedman's equation comes in:

$$CQ + PQ > IQ$$

Curiosity Quotient plus Passion Quotient is more important than Intelligence Quotient

Let's get started on those skills.

Guided or Free Writing Prompts

Writing prompts can be about dates of historical events or birthdays of famous individuals. But they can also be about letting the student's imagination fly. About giving them the confidence to start writing down what's on their mind.
Their five minute free writing exercises should *not* be corrected, but they can be shared by individuals reading their work to the classroom, if desired. If you are looking for more ideas, do an online search for 'creative writing prompts' and you'll find plenty.

- If I were going to be stranded on a desert island, what *ten* items would I want in my pockets?
- Chocolate makes me think about going far beyond the...
- How would you spend a found $10 bill?
- What is your earliest memory? Why has it stayed with you?
- I am happy with myself. Because...
- What does freedom taste like?
- What does freedom smell like?
- Everyday is Sunday. What do you think?
- I woke up this morning and I am a squirrel...
- My dream come true is...
- I want to live in the ___ century. Why?
- What happened?
- Who are we?

Poetry Exercises

As a species, we seem to be built to create poetry. It's all around us, in our music and in our everyday language. When we need to express emotion, it is the form we naturally use.

A good place to start with your students is to have them write poems that use imagery, then poems that use metaphors, and then poems that use couplets. Students seem to be naturally drawn to writing in rhymed couplets. Maybe it's the Dr. Seuss influence:

> I do not like them, Sam-I-am.
> I do not like green eggs and ham.

Or maybe it's the Biggie Smalls influence:

> kick in tha door wavin' tha 44
> all you heard was poppa don't hit me no more.

Or maybe it's a combination of them both…and of others who preceded them.

There are two kinds of couplets that you can have fun with:
- ➢ the **closed** couplet
- ➢ the **open** couplet

They sound more daunting than they really are…

In the **closed** couplet, the idea or image is complete at the end of the second line. One line can end without punctuation and run from the first line into the second line, but one closed couplet generally does not run into the next without punctuation.

Open couplets are more difficult to understand for some youngsters. An open couplet is the opposite of the closed couplet. An open couplet **cannot** stand alone. The sense or meaning of the poem may be carried from one couplet into the next. For example:

> That's my last duchess painted on the wall,
> Looking as if she were alive. I call
> That piece a wonder now: Fra Pandolf's hands
> Worked busily a day, and there she stands.
>
> –Robert Browning's *My Last Duchess*

This is only a part of Browning's poem, which is about the *murder* of the last duchess for smiling too much (sort of!). Note how the end of the second line (the end of the first couplet) runs into the second couplet. It needs the second couplet to complete its meaning ("…I call/ That piece a wonder…"). If you want to talk about this poem (it's on the following pages), point out the end rhyme (wall / call; hands / stands), and read it out loud to convey the consistent rhythm of the lines.

After writing closed and open couplets, the students will get a kick out of writing **ghazals**. For the purpose of these exercises, ghazals are poems made up of closed couplets that may be connected by a theme or topic, but "leap" in a structure that is non-linear and non-narrative. They are also a lot of fun to write as a group!

If you have a blackboard to write on, have the students write their poems on it as much as possible. Read each one and talk about the <u>strengths</u>. Don't be critical, and don't let anyone in the class be critical. Encourage. Incidentally, we (as a class) very often find ourselves laughing about these poems. Nothing wrong with that.

A couple of things to keep in mind…

- ➢ The poems produced in the imagery and metaphor exercises can be free verse or formal, it doesn't matter, at all.
- ➢ Contemporary couplets can be rhymed or unrhymed. It's up to the writer.
- ➢ Have fun.

New York State Standard 2.1   Language for Literary Response and Expression

Listening and reading for literary response involves comprehending, interpreting, and critiquing imaginative texts in every medium, drawing on personal experiences and knowledge to understand the text, and recognizing the social, historical and cultural features of the text.

Students (Intermediate):
- *read and view texts and performances from a wide range of authors, subjects, and genres*
- *identify significant literary elements …and use those elements to interpret the work*
- *recognize different levels of meaning*

Students (Commencement)
- *recognize and understand the significance of a wide range of literary elements and techniques, (including figurative language…) and use those elements to interpret the work*
- *understand how multiple levels of meaning are conveyed in a text*

New York State Standard 2.2

Speaking and writing for literary response involves presenting interpretations, analyses, and reactions to the content and language of a text. Speaking and writing for literary expression involves producing imaginative texts that use language and text structures that are inventive and often multilayered.

Students (Intermediate):
- *write stories, poems, literary essays, and plays that observe the conventions of the genre and contain interesting and effective language and voice*

Students (Commencement)
- *write original pieces in a variety of literary forms, correctly using the conventions of the genre and using structure and vocabulary to achieve an effect*

Poetry — Using Imagery

"Fire and Ice" by Robert Frost

Some say the world will end in fire,
Some say in ice.
From what I've tasted of desire
I hold with those who favor fire.
But if it had to perish twice,
I think I know enough of hate
To say that for destruction ice
Is also great
And would suffice.

Part 1

- Form groups of three or four.
- As I read Frost's "Fire and Ice" out loud, listen for certain images that appear in your mind. Turn the page over.
- As a group, use the paper to draw pictures (using no words) to explain and/or illustrate what Frost is saying in the poem. When sharing these with the class, have one group member hold up your depiction of Frost's poem and give the class a few seconds to try and guess how the picture(s) depict the poem.

Part 2

- Working individually now, take out a sheet of paper and a pen. Divide their paper into six squares.
- Each square will be filled with either a drawing or a word or phrase that will be an answer to the following prompts:
    - Draw one item from a knapsack.
    - Draw one item you would find in a car.

- o Draw one thing that you would find in a jungle.
- o Write a word/phrase that describes extreme heat.
- o Write a word/phrase that describes music.
- o Write a word/phrase that describes yourself.
➢ Next, write a poem with no limitations except that you use all (or at least five of the six) ideas that you drew or wrote down. This poem has no restrictions. No poetic devices are necessary; there is no set length; no set rhyme scheme, etc. It is open-ended, although use of such features is encouraged. You have ten minutes to write.
➢ After completing the poem, share with the class. If possible, write them on the board. As we read and hear each poem, we will guess which words describe the drawings of words/phrases of the previous activity of Part 2.

Further Writing: For the next meeting, compose 3-5 short poems that use imagery to create meaning. Bring them in to share with the class.

A couple of useful terms and their definitions:

Imagery—visually descriptive or figurative language in a literary work. It is also the pattern of images that run through a work.

Figurative language is a word or phrase that departs from everyday literal language for the sake of comparison, emphasis, clarity, or freshness.

Poetry — Using Metaphors #1

Definition: A metaphor is a comparison of two unlike things.

Part 1. Write your own metaphors for each of the following ideas or concepts. Make sure you know the exact meaning of the word.

Example: smallness

She was the spider, unnoticed by all, spinning her web among the endless, towering redwoods.

(Did you notice that the word 'smallness' is not used?)

1. loneliness

___

2. largeness

___

3. joyfulness

___

4. disgust

___

5. clarity

___

6. anger

_____
_____
_____

7. confusion

_____
_____
_____

8. excitement

_____
_____
_____

9. contentment

_____
_____
_____

10. optimism

_____
_____
_____

Part 2.

Choose two or more of the metaphors you have created and use them in creating 2-4 more poems.

Poetry—Using Metaphors #2

Read this poem out loud. Langston Hughes, the great African-American poet of the Harlem Renaissance, was a master in the use of metaphor.

"Dreams" by Langston Hughes

Hold fast to dreams
For if dreams die
Life is a broken-winged bird
That cannot fly.

Hold fast to dreams
For when dreams go
Life is a barren field
Frozen with snow.

Things to talk about:

- What are the two metaphors Langston Hughes uses?
- In the first metaphor, what is being compared to what?
- In the second metaphor, what is being compared to what?
- How do these metaphors help us understand the poet's feelings about "Dreams," the poem's title?
- How is using this metaphor different from simply saying that when dreams are unfulfilled life is difficult?
- What makes this an effective metaphor and why?

Writing Metaphor Poems

Write one or two poems of your own, using metaphor. You can even use Langston Hughes's topic, '"life's dreams,' if you want. Take your time and have fun with them. Don't worry about polishing them…yet. Still, feel free to revise them until they achieve the effect you want. Save each draft of the poem.

Poetry—Writing Closed Couplets

In the **closed** couplet, the idea or image is <u>complete</u> at the end of the second line. There may be enjambment (a line that ends without punctuation and runs from the first line into the second line), but one closed couplet does not enjamb into the next.

Here's a silly example we found online:

> Fish hooks floating through the sea,
> The little fish say, "Don't catch me!"
> Pulling, tugging on the line,
> Oh, no! Look! He is mine!

Short Imitation

In five minutes, write your own four-line poem (two sets of couplets). It can be funny or serious. Then share them with the class.

_____

_____

_____

_____

Writing more closed couplets

Think of a <u>season</u> or an <u>object in nature</u> to write about. Write a closed couplet on a sheet of notepaper. Put it away and do another in a few hours on the same subject on the same paper. Put it away and write another couplet an hour later. Write three more couplets at different times each day until the next meeting. Share what you've done.

Writing more closed couplets

A poem by Yvonne Blomer:

> Traffic noise, the constant hum,
> old oak, does it deafen?

Write your own poem by adding more couplets to Blomer's poem, copying the length of the lines and the position of punctuation, including asking a question of something in nature. Write as many couplets as you want. You may possibly want to finish your poem with some kind of answer to the questions. Share your poem.

NOTE: When you talk about the poems you are sharing, point out the good things you see or hear in the poems: the rhythm, the rhyme (if it has it), the clear image that paints a picture in your mind, comparisons (that we call metaphors) that add to the meaning (*"Germs are invisible assassins"* instead of *"Germs are deadly."*)

Writing Open Couplets

An **open** couplet is the opposite of the closed couplet. An open **couplet** cannot stand alone. The sense or meaning of the poem may be carried from one couplet into the next. For example:

> That's my last duchess painted on the wall,
> Looking as if she were alive. I call
> That piece a wonder now: Fra Pandolf's hands
> Worked busily a day, and there she stands.
>
> --Robert Browning's *My Last Duchess*

Look at how the end of the second line (the end of the first couplet) runs into the second couplet. It needs the second couplet to complete its meaning ("…I call/ That piece a wonder…").

Here is another example, taken from Lorna Crozier's selected poems *The Blue Hour of the Day*. Notice how many of the couplets need the next couplet to complete the meaning.

> **Falling In Love**
>
> The worst thing about
> a horse bite is the horse
>
> can't change his mind,
> can't open his mouth,
>
> release the flesh
> until his jaws clamp shut.
>
> Once the pain starts
> you know it has to
>
> get worse before
> it stops.

Writing Open Couplets

Write four to six open couplets. I don't mean to write one long sentence with only a period at the end. You may end a sentence in the middle of the line or at any point in a couplet that is linked to the previous one. Share them with the class.

Poetry—Writing Ghazals

The **ghazal** is a Persian form of poetry in couplets. North American ghazals tend to favor a feeling of "leaping" around. Often the subject matter of ghazals is love, both physical and mystical. Each couplet should focus on an image (a mental picture of something).

Ghazals have an essence to them that is characterized by a structure in which the couplets seem disconnected, but that seem to come together and mean something in the end. Here are the first four couplets from a ghazal by John Thompson.

> I know how small a poem can be:
> the point on a fish hook;
> women have one word or too many:
> I watch the wind;
> I'd like a kestrel's eye and know   kestrel=a small falcon
> how to hang on one thread of sky;
> the sun burns up my book:
> it must be all lies;

Writing Ghazals

Write a **ghazal** or a number of ghazals with 3-5 of your classmates. As a group, pick ONE of the following themes or topics: love, effort, fear, survival, hunger, history, happiness, family, evolution, jazz, superstition. Do not let the other groups know what topic you have chosen. Now, working separately for 2-3 minutes, each member of your group writes <u>one</u> closed couplet on that topic. When everyone has finished, put them together into one poem in one of two ways:

> ➢   Choose the couplets randomly and copy them down one after the other.

>   *or*

> ➢   As a group, organize the couplets in a way that feels right to you all.

Write your group's poem on the blackboard and have someone read it out loud. Have the class try to guess what the topic is and, as a group, talk about what in the poem effectively conveys something about the topic. Talk about whether there is a larger message that comes across. Seeing it on the board, do you think there is a better way to organize the ghazal?

Write a ghazal

Write a ghazal of your own of 6-10 couplets. Pick a topic and then let your mind find images from any number of sources. Think of music and places and movies and artwork and food smells and sports and history and home and books and… The key is let your mind "leap" around.

NOTES

Fiction

Storytelling has been part of every culture since the beginning of time. Over thousands of years, as humans struggled to survive, they have passed on their knowledge, their histories, and their beliefs to succeeding generations through the retelling of myths, legends, and folklore. Modern fiction carries on that tradition.

We are firm believers that individual growth goes hand in hand with being storytellers. In learning to become a fiction writer, students build problem-solving skills by planning the story. Their confidence rises as the words continue to pile up and they realize they are capable of finishing a project to the end. They learn to express their ideas clearly. They develop public speaking skills and build stronger vocabularies.

In this section, we will explore major elements of fiction:

- ➢ Character
- ➢ Plot
- ➢ Point of View
- ➢ Setting

We have also included exercises on using the senses to strengthen a story.

We will not specifically address short stories, but many of the same elements of the novel can be easily applied to them.

> A short story is confined to one mood, to which everything in the story pertains. Characters, setting, time, events, are all subject to the mood.
> –Eudora Welty

Most students need to start with short informal writing activities and work their way toward the creation of longer stories. Using prompts—like warm-up routine before playing a sport or a musical instrument—helps loosen up the imagination while honing the writing muscles.

Doing 5-7 minutes of freewriting every day, and keeping a journal is a good place to start.

New York State Standard 2.1   Language for Literary Response and Expression

Listening and reading for literary response involves comprehending, interpreting, and critiquing imaginative texts in every medium, drawing on personal experiences and knowledge to understand the text, and recognizing the social, historical and cultural features of the text.

Students (Intermediate):
- *read and view texts and performances from a wide range of authors, subjects, and genres*
- *identify significant literary elements …and use those elements to interpret the work*
- *recognize different levels of meaning*

Students (Commencement)
- *recognize and understand the significance of a wide range of literary elements and techniques, (including figurative language, imagery...) and use those elements to interpret the work*
- *understand how multiple levels of meaning are conveyed in a text*

New York State Standard 2.2

Speaking and writing for literary response involves presenting interpretations, analyses, and reactions to the content and language of a text. Speaking and writing for literary expression involves producing imaginative texts that use language and text structures that are inventive and often multilayered.

Students (Intermediate):
- *write stories, poems, literary essays, and plays that observe the conventions of the genre and contain interesting and effective language and voice*
- *produce literary interpretations of literary works that identify different levels of meaning and comment on their significance and effect [critiquing]*

Students (Commencement)
- *write original pieces in a variety of literary forms, correctly using the conventions of the genre and using structure and vocabulary to achieve an effect*
- *produce literary interpretations that explicate the multiple layers of meaning [critiquing]*

Writing Fiction—Using Senses and Imagination

The five senses are important for our writing. We use our sight sense so much for the images we describe as we write, but our writing improves if we can ground the reader in our fictional world through the use of other sensory images.

Here are some quick exercises to get warmed up.

Exercise: Pick an object and have students write descriptive words, using their five senses:

- sight, sound, smell, touch, taste

Any object around the classroom can be used for this exercise.

Example: Object is sand.

Looks like: *white, small, shiny.*
Feels like: *grainy, soft, slips through my fingers.*
Tastes like: *bitter, salty, tasteless.*
Sounds like: *quiet, rustle, silent.*
Smells like: *faint, odorless, sea.*

Exercise: Ask students to do a five-minute freewrite, answering the following prompts.

- If you had to lose one of your five senses, which would you choose? Why?

- Describe a "first" (first time driving a car, first lie, first big success, first roller coaster ride). Include as many details as possible, being sure to include an aspect relating to each of the five senses.

- You have entered your house on Thanksgiving Day. The turkey is burned. Follow the format of visual details, sound, smell, taste, and feel or touch.

Writing Fiction—Using Senses and Imagination

These are "freewriting" prompts for you to use for five days:

1. SOUND - Imagine that you are out windsurfing when a wild storm blows in. The waves are crashing in around and the other sounds of the storm are filling your ears as you tried desperately to get back to shore, where a line of rocks awaits. It is so dark and the waves so high that you can barely see anything. All you can hear are the sounds of the storm. Describe that experience to someone who has never been to the ocean.

2. SMELL - You are lying in bed on Saturday morning when you awaken to the aroma of coffee percolating and bacon frying. The phone rings and you begin to tell your friend about the smells of breakfast cooking. Then you smell something that you've never smelled before. Describe it.

3. TASTE - You and your sister decide to concoct a new drink. You mix all the carbonated drinks in the refrigerator into the blender. Then you add strawberries, bananas, tomatoes, and last night's leftover meatloaf. Last, you throw in a raw egg, a cup of milk, and some ice. As the blender crushes the mixture into a drink, you and your sister argue over who will have to taste it first. You lose. Describe the taste of that first swallow.

4. TOUCH - Ever touch a baby's skin? Describe how it feels. If you'd like, compare it to your own skin. How is it different?

5. SIGHT - Describe a sunset to a blind man who has never seen color.

Strive to use verbs that are descriptive, not just adjectives:

> Example: The scorching sun made our skin sweaty. ("made" isn't a very exciting verb.)
> Example: The scorching sun sizzled the sweat on our skin. ("sizzled" paints a more graphic picture.)

Settings Exercise

Close your eyes and imagine the perfect place. It can be a place close to you right now, or it could be a place in another time or in another dimension. Wherever it is, put yourself in the middle of it. Look in front of you and look behind you. Look up and down. See it and feel it clearly.

> ➢ Now take ten minutes and describe the place as fully as you can.

Settings Exercise #2

Questions to consider about the setting for your story.

What is the year, month, or day that the story begins?

Season?

Is that relevant?

Where?

Why is the story set here?

Why are the protagonists here?

- **Physical setting**

What is the climate? When (month) do the seasons change?

What's the topography (mountains, hills, ocean, lakes)?

Plants and animals that live here?

Special land forms or points of interest?

Natural obstacles that will help/hinder your protagonists?

How did your protagonists get here? How will they leave?

- **Social setting**

Population?

Types of dwellings?

Kinds of stores and businesses?

Ethnic make-up of the community?

Local industries/jobs?

Holidays?

Entertainment?

What current events might be important in your story?

- ➢ **Using setting in the story**

Write a one-line characterization of the setting.

Identify the trait that will make the setting come alive and explain why (e.g. isolated, bustling, hot...).

How do the characters feel about being where they are? Is this relevant to their actions?

Consider the atmosphere that you have created. What kind of characters might be there and what kind of "situation" might they be in?

- ➢ **Critiquing**

Swap your work with a partner. Read through the work. Consider the questions you asked yourself about your own work at the beginning of the exercise. Be ready to discuss the work with the class.

What positive things can you say about the work? BE SPECIFIC.

What could the writing do better? BE SPECIFIC.

Writing Fiction—Know Your Characters

Choose one of the main characters from your story. Write one or two word descriptions on the following: (The same exercise can be done on every character used in the short story or novel.)

Name:

Age:

Gender:

Hair color/Eye color:

Height:

Weight:

Profession:

Education:

Race/Ethnic Background:

Idiosyncrasies:

Favorite saying:

Write down three objectives (non-physical ones) that describe the character. Underline the dominate trait. (i.e. He wants to use his innate cunning to win a place on the team.)

1.

2.

3.

> **Questions to ask your character**:

Answer in first person. ***BECOME* your character**. This can be done in a group setting, where class members ask these questions.)

What do you love the most?

What drives you?

What are your strengths/weaknesses?

What are your inner fears?

What are your personal conflicts?

What's troubling you today?

What is the one thing in the world your character would do anything to have?

Why?

What is the one thing in the world your character would do anything to avoid?

Why?

How do you treat others?

What are your faults/flaws?

In what way are you vulnerable?

What is your deep, dark secret?

Write a brief bio about that character, include the following kinds of information:

- job/profession
- religious affiliation
- type of personality
- type of car
- how many siblings
- any other info you'd like to share with us...

Advance tips on character development

Create 'special' protagonists and worthy opponents.

If there is one element that can make or break a story, it is character development. First things first, though. The reader has to care about the characters. Moreover, many beginning writers make the mistake of inventing intelligent, clever protagonists, but then pit them against simple villains. The match of wits should be fairly even, or the conflict and tension will be contrived.

- Every character (including the villain) should have a goal and something personal at stake in the emerging conflict. Keep this goal in mind at all times for consistent motivation. For the story to come alive, every character must think the story is really about *them*.

- Every character should have a few key strengths that mold and form them. For example: the genius, the athlete, the military man. Don't give them too many strengths or they will be unbelievable.

- Every character should have some vulnerability. This will take your characters from cardboard cutouts to being real human beings.

- Every character should have a moral code…the things they will and will not do. Everyone has boundaries, and these boundaries should shape the characters in the emerging story.

- Everyone must evolve. Conflict and obstacles and setbacks in a story are like fire, breaking down your characters and forging better, stronger people in their place. Jaded characters, burned by relationships, learn to love; loners to trust. The protagonist and the antagonist impact each other, bend each other, and reshape each other permanently.

Writing Fiction—Plot

We consider plot a road map. How to go from A to Z.

A plot is a creative plan for a story involving a sequence of events from beginning to middle to end. In simple terms, a plot is the writer's plan for what happens when and to whom. The events usually follow a pattern: a situation is established; a conflict or problem arises, certain events bring about a climax, and the conflict is resolved. Here is some brief information on key elements:

Conflict

- The writer develops a conflict—a struggle between opposing forces. This conflict creates tension and suspense in a story. There can be one or many conflicts.
    - External Conflict. A character struggles with some outside person or force.
    - Internal Conflict. In this type of conflict, a struggle takes place within the mind of the character. Moral questions. Right or wrong. Guilt.

Climax

- The climax takes place when the reader experiences the greatest emotional response to a character's problem, and that problem is resolved at this point, one way or another. A decisive action needs to be made to end the basic conflict.

Resolution

- The resolution is the point at the end of the story where loose ends are tied up.

General Guidelines for Plot Building

- Let characters influence the plot. Think about the characters in a particular situation, and plot ideas will emerge.

- Avoid too much plot. Don't create a crisis every couple of pages, too many characters and story lines, etc. Short stories are generally about ONE event that your protagonist is about to face, is facing, or has just faced.

- Start in the middle of the action. The story should begin with the characters moving forward. For example, a story about a family coping with the breakup of the parents' marriage might begin on the day one parent moves out.

- Let readers wait. Anticipation is part of the fun for readers. Readers get involved because they want to know what happens to the characters. If you answer that question too soon, you may have to dream up another plot to finish the story.

- Pace the plot. Think of your plot as having a kind of wave motion: with ups and downs, action sequences, and tension that builds up, comes to a crest, and then settles down. This kind of pacing sets your reader up for the final climax.

- Let your characters grow. In most stories, plot is about how life affects people or characters. Between the beginning and the end of your story, your main characters should learn, grow, and be in some way changed by the events they have just lived through.

Many plotting techniques and methods exist and are used by writers:
- storyboarding
- Three-Act Structure
- the Hero's Journey
- many more

None of these things are new. Each writer has to find what works for him or her. We will get into more detail on two methods that we frequently use ourselves, the Three-Act Structure and the Hero's Journey.

Plot—Three-Act Structure

The plots of many movies and television shows are built in three parts or acts. It is not complicated; even Sesame Street teaches this to pre-schoolers. Having three acts allows the writer to pace the action effectively, and keep it focused.

Three-Act Structure

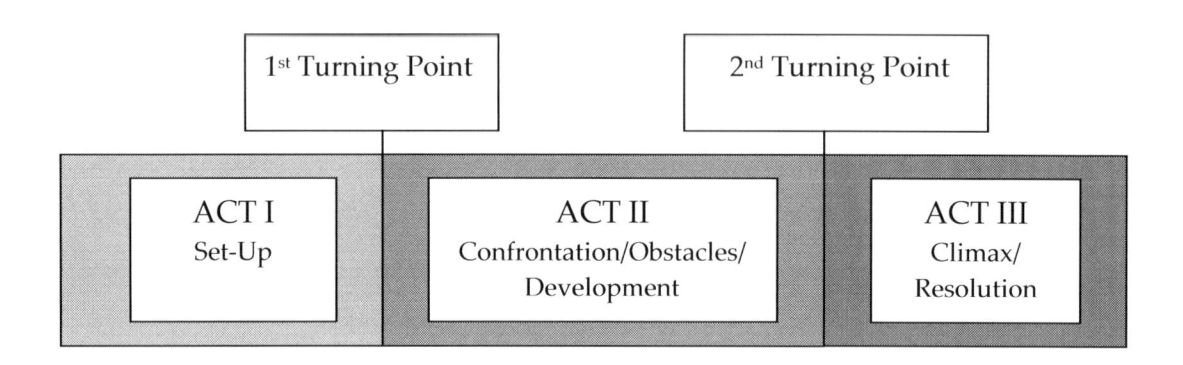

```
         1st Turning Point              2nd Turning Point

   ┌──────────────┬──────────────────────────┬──────────────┐
   │   ACT I      │        ACT II            │   ACT III    │
   │   Set-Up     │ Confrontation/Obstacles/ │   Climax/    │
   │              │      Development         │  Resolution  │
   └──────────────┴──────────────────────────┴──────────────┘
```

> **Act I:**

Also known as the 'set-up.' We must give the reader *just* the important info needed to start the story. For example: characters and the setting of the story. Also the writer should introduce the *central question* that will be resolved at the climax. Remember Act I doesn't need to convey *everything*. In most good films, for example, the set-up begins with an image. This visual picture gives us a strong sense of the place, the mood, and sometimes the theme. Act I is about 25% of the story and ends at the First Turning Point.

> **First Turning Point:** The story kicks into gear, and we get the story question: Will the protagonist win? Get what he or she wants? Survive?

> **Act II:**

This is the main part of the story that presents character development. In this section protagonist works on confronting the antagonist in ever-escalating conflicts. The second act is about 50% of the story and often, during this part, the protagonist learns new skills through these confrontations, preparing him or her for the Second Turning Point.

> **Second Turning Point:** Some action occurs that causes the story to ratchet up as outcomes of decisions become even more critical.

> **Act III:**

Climax and Resolution: The major action that created the Second Turning Point finishes Act II, and now the stakes are raised regarding both the characters and the central question that needs to be resolved. The action speeds up, sometimes by using shorter scenes, but with enough development that the readers' emotions are fully engaged right up to a clearly defined climax—where the central question is finally resolved. A quick wrap-up then ties up loose ends…or sends the reader off with an insight they need to think about.

Here is another, more detailed depiction of the same concept.

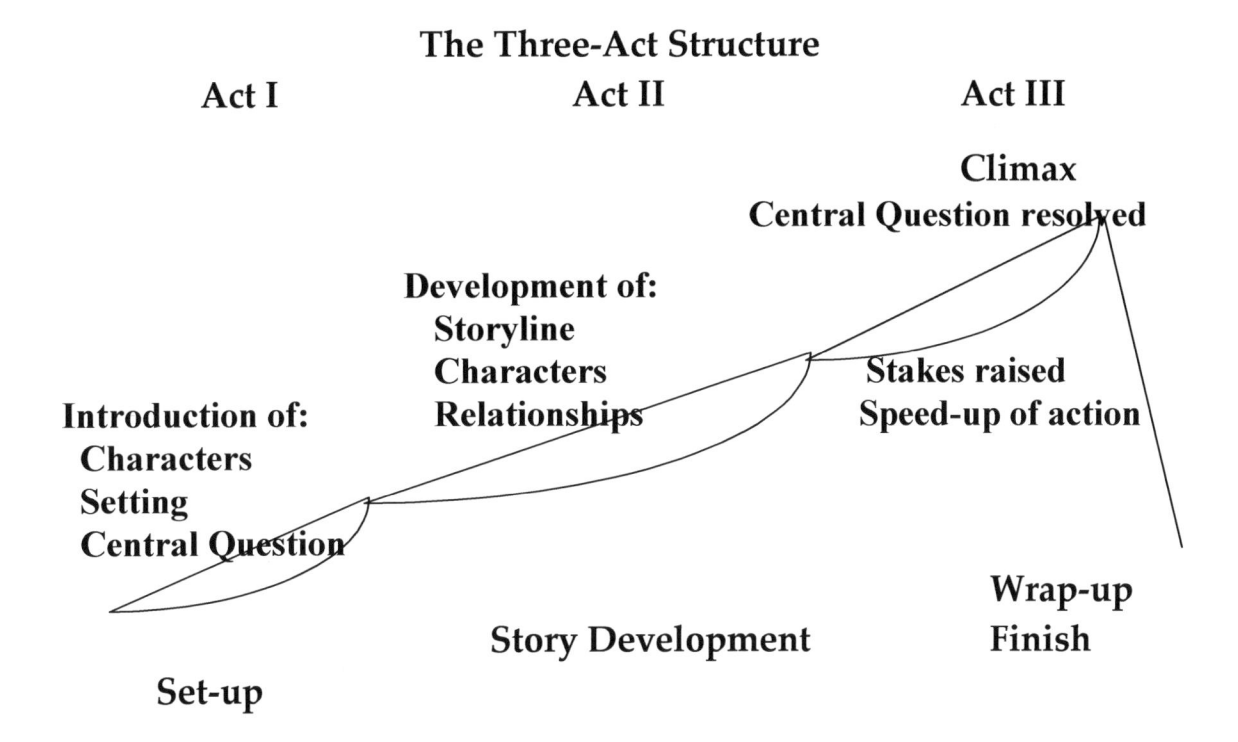

The Three-Act Structure

Act I   **Act II**   **Act III**

Climax
Central Question resolved

Development of:
Storyline
Characters   **Stakes raised**
Relationships   **Speed-up of action**

Introduction of:
Characters
Setting
Central Question

               Wrap-up
       Story Development   **Finish**

Set-up

Plot: The Hero's Journey

The Hero's Journey is a plot structure that the large number of successful stories and Hollywood movies are based upon. It actually is based on the development of the protagonist into a hero. Many writing teachers refer to it, but the Hero's Journey originates in the work of a man named Joseph Campbell, who studied the similarities of thousands of stories and myths. Here are the steps:

Call to Adventure:

- ➢ Introducing the hero's status, capabilities, nature, ordinary world, inner challenge, outer challenge, and more. The story begins in the ordinary world. Here, of course, we meet the hero and his problems. This is how we can introduce the story question—the protagonist's underlying quest. Then comes the *Call to Adventure*. A herald arrives, announcing the change. The "We need YOU" call.

Refusal of the Call:

- ➢ Normally, the hero isn't interested. Obviously, this is going to be hard work, and maybe he or she doesn't want to find their place in the world that badly. This is the *Refusal of the Call*. Fear doesn't have to be the only reason for being reluctant—he may also have noble reasons, or perhaps other characters are preventing him from leaving.

Supernatural Aid:

- ➢ A mentor (like a Dumbledore or a Gandolf or an Obi-Wan) is sought to provide advice, training, guidance, direction, magical gifts, and more. This can take place after the hero has committed to the adventure.

First Threshold:

- ➢ This is where the hero leaves the ordinary world and enters the new, special world. This is where our hero faces his first test, the first challenge to his commitment. Life will never be the same once the hero passes the threshold. Often this crossing of the threshold is the First Turning Point of the story.

The bulk of the story comes in the following steps, *which can come in any order*. Some writing teachers call it the 'Tests, Allies and Enemies Stage.' Here, the hero meets lots of people and has to determine whether they're allies or enemies. Sometimes, mistakes are made…

Transformation. Also known as The Road of Trial:
- Transformation can include growing, learning, maturing or similar.

Seizing the Sword:
- The hero finds and seizes the sword or instrument needed to complete the quest.

Rebirth through Death and Reward:
- The hero is tempted into place where he undergoes a near-death experience.

Atonement:
- The hero confronts his or her limitations.

The Elixir:
- The hero takes possession of the magic elixir.

Return with the Elixir:
- The hero gets back on the road home, but faces more trials and battles.

Rescue from Without:
- An outside force appears at a critical moment to aid the hero in completing the quest.

Apotheosis:
- The hero attains illumination and insight, and becomes transformed into the best he or she can be.

Final Ordeal:
- ➢ This ordeal or battle pushes the hero to the limit. The climax often occurs during this stage. Remember that the hero realizes he has changed. Here, we get to see that change in action. If this is the climax, then *this* is where the hero finally triumphs over the antagonist.

Crossing the Return Threshold:
- ➢ The hero returns to the ordinary world triumphant. Here we have the denouement. We wrap up all the loose threads. Characters receive their rewards or punishments.

After this, the hero may leave the ordinary world because once he has become transformed into the Master of Two Worlds, he may no longer feel he belongs in the place where he began. Frodo Baggins in *Lord of the Rings* is a great example of this.

Writing Fiction — the Connection between Character Development and Plot

Exercise: Discuss the Hero's Journey in terms of a book or movie that you know (*Spiderman, Twilight, I Am Legend, Law Abiding Citizen, Taken, Astro Boy…*). How many steps does the hero take that are similar?

- *Call to Adventure*
- *Reluctance to answer the Call*
- *Supernatural Aid…a mentor or a magic talisman*
- *Crossing the First Threshold*
- *Transformation…the Road of Trial*
- *Seizing the Sword*
- *Rebirth through Death and Reward*
- *Atonement*
- *Taking possession of the Elixir*
- *Return with the Elixir*
- *Rescue from Without*
- *Apotheosis*
- *Final Ordeal*
- *Crossing the Return Threshold*

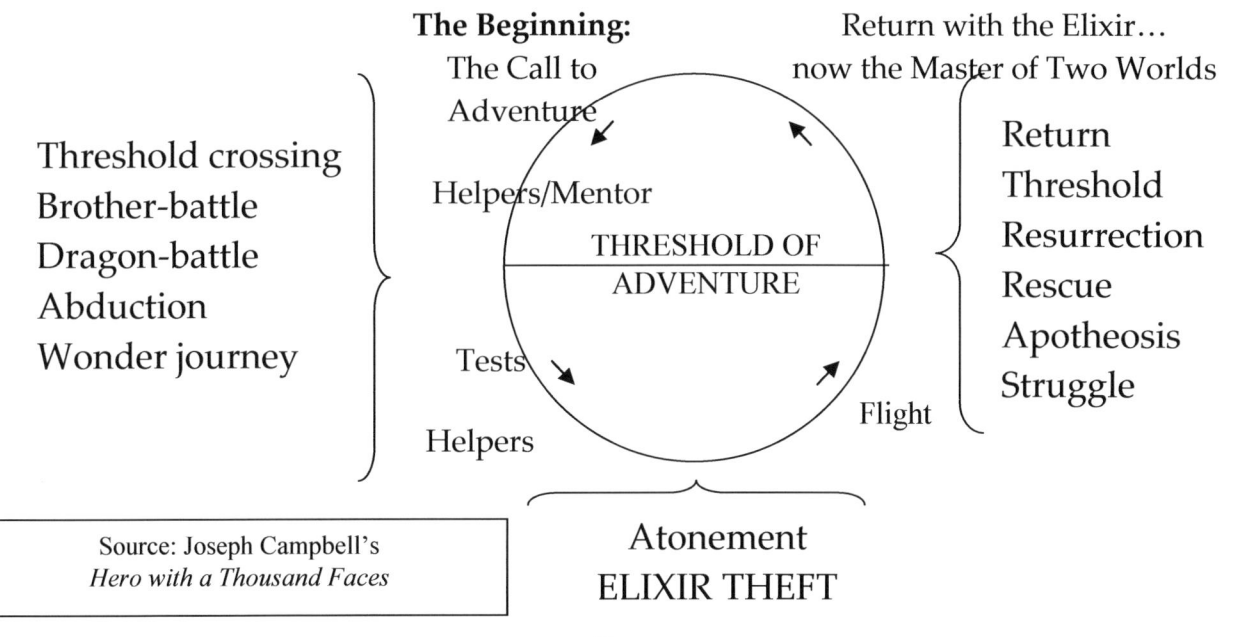

The Beginning: The Call to Adventure

Return with the Elixir… now the Master of Two Worlds

Threshold crossing
Brother-battle
Dragon-battle
Abduction
Wonder journey

Helpers/Mentor

THRESHOLD OF ADVENTURE

Tests
Helpers

Flight

Return Threshold
Resurrection
Rescue
Apotheosis
Struggle

Atonement
ELIXIR THEFT

Source: Joseph Campbell's *Hero with a Thousand Faces*

Fiction—Point of View

Point of View (POV) is often thought of as a movie camera where the reader can see and hear a story, depending on where the camera is located. In literary terms, POV describes the perspective from which a piece of fiction is told. Remember that a single work of fiction can have many narrators and many points of view.

The trick, as the writer, to finding the right POV is striking this balance between intimacy and perspective. You want readers to care about your characters and understand how they experience the world.

Most of the time, fiction writers choose either first-person narration or third-person narration. A first-person narrator speaks as 'I.' Narration in the third person describes action from a more detached perspective. In third person narration, characters will be referred to by their names or the third-person pronouns (he, she, and they).

➢ **Subjective Point of View, Objective Point of View**

Objective POV is like a security camera, hanging overhead, recording the action that takes place within range of its lens. It reveals information without having an opinion. Objective narrators act as observers rather than opinionated participants.

Subjective POV is like having the camera attached to top of one character's head. The readers see and hear the action from that character's perspective. The reader can also hear the character's thoughts, if the author chooses to share it.

Subjective narrators generally are limited in what they know (limited omniscient) because they offer only one of many possible perspectives on the action they describe.

Exercise: Read a well-known fairy tale to the class, like "Goldilocks and the Three Bears" or "Little Red Riding Hood." Decide whose perspective the story is told from. Then have students retell the story from the POV of one of the other characters in the story.

Share them in the class.

Critiquing

The English playwright John Osborne said, "Asking a writer what he thinks about criticism is like asking a lamppost what it feels about dogs."

But we all need feedback on our writing. This is especially true in fiction. Critiquing is a two-way process. If it's a buddy system or putting our work on display for everyone in the class to read and comment on, we need to learn how to both give and take criticism.

Here are some things to remember when giving critique:

Be Positive:
- ➢ Always try to come up with something positive to say about the piece you are reviewing. By that, we don't mean non-comments, such as: "I like it!" or "This is good." These sentences are good for the ego but don't help the writer in any way. Instead of general comments, be specific about the characters or dialogue or setting, for example. Giving a critique isn't all about the things that are wrong with a piece of writing; it is also about finding and praising what is good. Knowing what they have done well also helps writers to develop.

Be Honest:
- ➢ Don't say that the work is perfect if it isn't. This kind of non-critique is of no use whatsoever. People put their work up for feedback and critiques in order to improve their writing. Don't be afraid to point out where mistakes have been made, but do remember to be positive first, and then to focus on the writing.

Be careful about choice of words:
- ➢ Think about the person receiving the critique. Don't start any sentences that begin with 'you.' You don't want the writer to feel he or she is being personally attacked. You are critiquing the work, not the writer. Try to start sentences with words such as 'I' or 'The.' For example, avoid saying things like, "You have got to be kidding me! Have you EVER heard a retired English professor talk? This character sounds more like Spud, your brother-in-law, who I know for a fact has never read a book in his life!" Instead, you might say, "I like the fact that you bring the professor into this scene, but maybe his character's speech patterns should include more formal words. That way, he'll sound more like a retired English professor." Focus on the product.

What to Look For When Giving a Critique

Here's a list of things you can and should look for when critiquing someone's work.

- Does the story start in the right place?
- Does the story have an interesting hook?
- Does the story *show* what is happening (good) or simply *tell* what is happening (not good)?
- Is the dialogue sound realistic for each speaker in the story? Does it help move the plot along?
- Plot. Is it believable?
- Is the conflict believable?
- Pacing of the story. Are you drawn into the action and kept interested?
- Is each individual scene necessary?
- The setting. Is there just enough description to ground the reader?
- Point of View. Is it consistent?
- Final editing stuff—grammar, spelling, punctuation. Is it right?

You don't have to comment on everything. Look for things that stand out. Comment on them.

Do try to give feedback on what could be changed to improve the piece. We all have our own styles and our own tastes. That is not relevant, and we should respect the writer's style and taste. Be specific…offer examples as suggestions.

Never criticize the author, only provide criticism of the work.

Things to Remember When Receiving a Critique:

- Take time to thank the person who has done the critique. Reading and providing feedback on works can take a long time.
- Do think carefully about the comments that have been made.
- Don't immediately fire back defensive messages. Take time to re-read your work and consider the comments made about it.
- Do take the time to critique other people's work, too.

Critiquing isn't hard. It does, however, take time and practice.

Creative Nonfiction

According to Phil Druker of the University of Idaho, creative nonfiction is a mixture of factual information and good storytelling. He defines the genre this way:

- It is a hybrid of literature and nonfiction.
- The author tells a story (entertains the readers), presents factual information (expands readers' knowledge of the subject), and shares passion for the topic.
  - The trick is to balance these three elements to make the text work for the readers. Too much or not enough of either one can weaken the piece.
- It presents a whole picture of the subject and recognizes the complexity of the world/ the limits of what we can know.
- It presents a way of looking at the world:
  - concrete examples, narration
  - grounded in self
  - interesting to the reader (and writer)
  - unique voice
- It presents documentable subject matter—grounded in real-world facts and issues.
- It presents useful, interesting facts based on exhaustive research.
- The facts come alive through narration and setting—or well-developed scenes.
- It presents details that help the reader understand the main point.
- It focuses on showing rather than telling.

"Guidelines for Writing Creative NonFiction" comes from Barbara Lounsberry:

- Research thoroughly.
- Cultivate relationships with your subjects over a period of time to create trust, absorb information, note change, and know individuals so you can describe their thoughts, feelings, and attitudes correctly.
- Never invent or change facts or events. The truth is stranger than fiction.
- Avoid composites.
- Aim for a clear style with rhythm, "texture," color, and a dramatic pace.
- Write for real people to enrich their lives.
- Write about real events and people to make them come alive and record them.
- "Have faith in the value and importance of human being and human events..."

And Druker's goals of creative nonfiction:
- Deal with an issue/problem people are concerned about or find a way to make them concerned or interested.
- Give your readers new information to help them understand themselves, the world better.
  - Give background to educate your readers.
  - Provide accurate data.
  - Be truthful. Be honest.
  - Research thoroughly and carefully (the more you look, the more you'll find).
  - Use a variety of sources:
    - primary (interviews, trips to the place, personal experience, surveys)
    - secondary (library research . . . .)
- Consider your audience.
  - Use fiction techniques to draw the reader in:
    - narration
    - characterization
    - setting/place
    - personal involvement
  - Use interesting language.
- Cite your sources so readers know how you gathered the information.
- Report fairly.
  - Be objective.
  - Be logical.
  - Select information carefully.
  - Provide details.
  - Use facts, real people, real situations. Be frank. Don't be too personal.
- Interpret your information.
  - Introduce
  - Give facts, examples, quotations . . .
  - Analyze, interpret, explain, synthesize.
- Draw conclusions.
- Organize your information.
  - Put your information in a logical order (chronological, spatial, dramatic, general to specific. . . .).
  - Put your information in an interesting order.
  - Use clear paragraphs (topic/purpose).
    Deal with information in blocks.
  - Consider using headings.

Writing Creative Nonfiction

Creative nonfiction (also known as literary or narrative nonfiction) is a type of writing that uses the same techniques used in fiction writing, but to create *factually accurate* narratives. Creative nonfiction is different from other nonfiction, such as technical writing or journalism, which is also rooted in accurate fact but is not primarily written in service as 'art.'

For a text to be considered creative nonfiction, it must be factually accurate, and written with attention to literary style and technique. "Ultimately, the primary goal of the creative nonfiction writer is to communicate information, just like a reporter, but to shape it in a way that *reads like fiction*." Forms of creative nonfiction include:

- personal essays
- memoir (tells about an important period of time in your life)
- travel writing
- food writing
- biography
- literary journalism
- and other hybridized essays

Critic Chris Anderson claims that creative nonfiction can be understood best by splitting it into two subcategories—the *personal* essay and the *journalistic* essay—but right now (according to *Wikipedia*) creative nonfiction simply does not have an established definition.

Exercise: Your task is to produce a personal essay that follows the format of NPR's "This I Believe." It can be about anything. The focus on the assignment will be on your personal *voice*. Use your craft to create a written work that allows the reader to hear YOU in the words.

To start, go to the NPR website http://www.npr.org/templates/story/story.php?storyId=4538138. Read about the project, browse through the essays, and read four or five very carefully. Choose a few essays that are very different. You'll find essays by everyone from soldiers in Afghanistan to the person who lives up the block from you to Muhammad Ali to dead presidents. As you read or listen to the essays (yes, because they were broadcast on the radio, they are available to listen to) pay attention to how the writers use language to express themselves…to put themselves on the page.

The length will be limited to about 500 words…only about two or three pages. Keep this in mind as you plan what you want to write.

Begin to write it in class. When you have a paragraph, stop and write it on the board. Get some feedback on your topic. If you are writing about a trip you made to a little village in Puerto Rico where your family is from, or about a frightening experience that shaped your own beliefs in some way, or about the happiest holiday of your life, see what your classmates have to say about it. They might even have suggestions about how you can shape your essay.

Note: Anyone can submit their essay for consideration to be published by NPR (with the writer reading their own essay), but you'll need your parent's permission if you are under 18.

Bring the creative nonfiction piece in to post on a board where your classmates can read it.

Have fun!

Writing Creative Nonfiction

For your second creative nonfiction piece, choose one of these other kinds of writing:

- memoir
- travel writing
- food writing
- biography
- literary journalism

This time, think about crafting your essay with the skills you learned about writing fiction.

- How can you use what you know about plot to create the sense of rising action and a climactic moment?
- How can you use settings to ground your reader in this true story you are telling?
- How can you use sensory images to make the reading experience more vivid and exciting?
- How about the use of metaphors?
- Or the use of rhythms and rhymes that you learned writing poetry?

The topic can be about an environmental issue or a neighborhood hero…the best ethnic food in the world or a battle between two ants on your front steps…the kindness of a stranger or an ugliest pet pageant…or whatever. **This essay is all yours**. But limit the length to about 500 words again!

Once again, if you start this in class, consider talking with your classmates about possible topics…and directions to go with a topic or ways to craft it.

Bring it in and post it for others to enjoy!

Publishing the Student's Work

After each term, Jim publishes a soft cover literary journal-style collection of student work. The online company he uses is Lulu.com. Students take responsibility for cover design and for editing the work. The step-by-step procedure is very simple and is well laid out on the publisher's webpage. The final product is a showcase of the students' work for their peers, parents, teachers, and administrators. And the cost is funded by grants through local supporters of arts. It is very inexpensive.

Another online company he has used is Createspace.com. CreateSpace is owned by Amazon, so as part of their publishing contract, the work will be available for sale on Amazon.com. This is acceptable to some school districts but not acceptable to others.

Either way—available for public purchase or not available for public purchase—Jim has parents sign a waiver, giving their okay for their child's work and name being included in the publication.

There are also online sources where students can list their work to be shared or to be critiqued. Some websites simply provide an interactive community of other writers.

Here is a list of just a few of them. Check them out and see if they work for you.

- Teen Central—Teen Central is a place where students can submit their stories about their lives. They can also read other writer's stories about things teens face in everyday life. The works are totally anonymous.
    - http://www.teencentral.net/

- Live Journal—For students who like to keep a journal or read other people's, then Live Journal is for them. They can create and customize their own online journal and write whenever they feel in it. It can be private or public.
    - http://www.livejournal.com/

- Teen Ink Magazine—Teen Ink is a magazine written by teens for teens. It features reviews, contests, interviews, galleries, poems and fiction. Join the Student Advisory Board or submit your work.
    - http://www.teenink.com/

Articles for Creative Writers

Writing a Nonfiction Book Proposal

or

Something Productive for Teachers to Do During Faculty Meetings

...and for Administrators to Do During School Board Meetings

We start this article with the assumption that you have a topic about which you are fairly knowledgeable. This is why you are reading this article. Nonfiction books represent a huge part of the book market. They sell on the basis of an idea, a table of contents, and sample chapters, even for unpublished writers...if there is something you can sell yourself as being an expert at. The potential payoff? Good money and a great credential for your publication record.

But is it that simple? Well, there are lots of good books out there giving you detail instructions, but here is an eight-step process that we followed, adapted from Michael Larsen's awesome book *How to Write a Book Proposal*.

Step 1   Pre-Writing: Resources—Information vs. Expertise

If you are not an expert, then become one by reading extensively on whatever your topic might be. The more you learn, the more you earn. Read the competitive books and complementing books. This provides information you need when writing the proposal.

Step 2   Pre-Writing: Shaping a marketable idea

Test-market your idea by...

1. Giving talks or workshops about it. Parts of the presentation can become chapters in your book, and making presentations on your topic will also enable you to:

    ➢ Build your passion for the subject.

- Receive instant feedback based on how your audiences respond.
- Generate humor, anecdotes, and ideas for your book through your audiences' comments.
- Build advance publicity and a market for the book. There is nothing like word of mouth in publishing.
- See if you enjoy talking about the subject enough to make it a part of your life. In the case of non-fiction topics, the publisher will want you to be out there marketing the book.
- Predict, by the number of people who come out to hear you, the reception that awaits the book.
- Increase your credibility.
- Build your professional network.
- Impress potential agents and editors.
- Develop your confidence.
- Explore the use of an advance order form to hand sell the book (once you have a publisher and you are approaching the publication date).

2. Writing articles about your topic. You not only reach a wider audience, but increase your command of your information.

3. Thinking through the possibility of publishing the book yourself. Though this seems out of place in a test-marketing stage, don't ignore the possibility of going this route. Some nonfiction books that were self-published first…The One-Minute Manager, What Color is Your Parachute?, The Celestine Prophecy, The Christmas Box.

Step 3   Pre-Writing: The Angle—Finding the HOOK

This is that mysterious element that engages the interest of agent, editor, and reader. Our recommendation is not to exaggerate the value of your book (e.g., "This book will revolutionize the way America eats" or "Our step-by-step method will increase productivity by 100% in just two weeks.") Remember, too, that anecdotes humanize an idea's appeal. Lastly, think of a catchy title that is descriptive, too. One that will sell and tell.

Step 4 Pre-Writing: The whole book packaging concept—Knowing the potential publisher, buyer, and product

Art books, textbooks, heavily illustrated medical and scientific books. A packager is an individual or company that has an idea for a book. The packager pitches the idea to a publisher, obtains a contract, then hires a writer to execute the text. Then the packager may or may not (depending on the deal) rewrite the manuscript, edit it, and supply everything from illustrations to cover art, mechanicals, film, marketing support, etc.. You, too, should have a good clear idea of how the book will physically look, consist of in terms of text and illustrations, etc., and be marketed.

Step 5 Proposal-Writing: The query letter—Perhaps the most critical part of any proposal: format, content, and hook in a sales document

The query letter is perhaps the most critical part of any proposal. If it works, the editor or agent will turn the page and read the rest of your proposal. If it doesn't work...well, you could have the best book out there, but no one will get anywhere near reading it.

So consider in writing the query letter that you:

- Make sure the query is of the highest quality. No mistakes of any kind—grammar, punctuation, etc.. You are selling yourself as a professional in this letter.
- Address the letter to a live person. Take the time to find out who is the acquiring editor.
- A clear opening is key! Try to give a visual image of your proposal.

    An example:

    Dear Ms. Barnett:

    In the fiction world, more and more people are trying to write with a partner. We are proposing a book on the topic for Heinemann's list of publications for writers.

- Keep it to one page.
- Mention any connection you may have with the addressee.

- Give the work's approximate length, the target market, and the estimated completion date (if you're not done with it, yet).

- Toot your own horn... (i.e., "The award-winning author of [so many] short stories") Publication is publication. Mention it.

Step 6 Proposal-Writing: Presentation—Making it look professional.

Most proposals range from 35 to 70 pages. There is no single way of doing it…just as there is no single way to write a book…but make it crackle with energy and professionalism.

Step 7 Proposal-Writing: Format and Content

1. Title page. Consists of: Title of proposal, Name, Address, Agent name, Phone number, e-mail address. (That's ALL!)

2. Resume. If you have an impressive resume, put it after title page. If not, put it in as the last page of the proposal package.

3. Table of Contents. This is for the proposal and not for the proposed book. For example:
    Overview--- page 1
    Market and Competition---page 2, etc.

   Make sure your name and the title of the book show up on this page.

4. Overview. Very important since it sells or rejects the book. Usually the overview should start with a three-line, high concept description of the book.

   In our proposal for MARRIAGE OF MINDS: Collaborative Fiction Writing, *the Overview starts with:*

   "Collaboration enhances creativity! How else would the human race continue to propagate itself? Why, even Dolly the sheep (of the Clan MacClone) is the product of collaborative scientific effort! The same holds for writing...."

5. Market and competition—Tell what other books of this type are out there…and why this one is different. Do research. Tell them exactly what's out there,

including author names, pages, years of publication. They may very well know, and they'll be impressed with your knowledge of the market.

6. Specifications—Your vision of the length, format, layout, number of chapters, pages, illustrations, special organizational schemes. Guestimate! Make it sound as if you know. ☺

7. Promotions and author bio—ways to market the work. Associations, newsletters, conferences. Where and how YOU can help. Be an active resource. Also, list your expertise on the topic. Professional, vocational credits.

8. Outline—explanation of each chapter, with a breakdown of how many pages per chapter. The rule of thumb: for every page in the chapter there should be one sentence of description in each chapter section. (We believe you can get away with less, however.).

Step 8   Proposal-Writing: The sample chapter

This is a critical element in making the proposal a successful selling tool. Pick out (or write) a chapter that provides the potential publisher with the flavor of the book. Don't include an introductory chapter that gives the organization of the book.

There you have it. Get writing.

Who Am I, and What Am I Missing?

Assessing Our Needs as Writers

No matter where we are in our writing vocation—regardless of how many stories we have in our heads or how many books we have written—the time always comes when we ask ourselves, "Why we are not moving on to that next step?"

Well, after going to the corner psychic, the next thing we recommend is doing a survey of your strengths and weaknesses. And believe us, this is much easier than Madame Rouge's suggestion to bury a live chicken up to its neck in the neighbor's yard by the light of a full moon!

So how do we take an inventory of our skills?

To prepare, look back at any writing that you've done. The purpose of this is not to depress you or to pump up your ego. We simply want you to look as honestly as possible at yourself *as a writer*. What are your strengths? What are your weaknesses? Then jot down answers to these questions…

1. Generating Ideas
   Are you one of those people with a constant surge of ideas? When you read the paper, watch the news, watch people in a mall, do you often ask, *what if*?

2. Inventing and Developing Characters
   Is it easy for you to create the people in your fiction? Do you know what they look like? Do you know their past, present, and future? Do you feel their pain, their motivation, their aspirations? Do your characters talk back to you? (If you answered yes to the last question, you may need a therapist.)

3. Creating Conflict
   Do your characters have identifiable internal and external conflicts? Is their conflict more than a mere misunderstanding that can be resolved by simply talking it out? Will the resolution of their internal conflict directly enable them to resolve their external conflict?

4. Plotting

    Do you like creating detailed plots? Are you familiar with plotting techniques? Do you have the ability to see a beginning, middle, and end to your story before you begin to write? Do you have enough key points of action built into your novel to keep the reader turning the pages?

5. Creating subplots

    As with plot, are you able to see a beginning, middle, and end in your subplots? Do you have the ability to weave the subplots effectively into your story?

6. Dialogue

    How effective are you in writing dialogue? Are you able to create different voices for the different characters in your novel? Can you capture diverse feelings in the course of a conversation?

7. Description

    Can you use descriptive language to effectively depict what you have personally experienced? Can you effectively describe what you have researched, but never seen (as in historical fiction)? Can you effectively conjure the language to describe what you have never seen (or what may not even exist—as in fantasy, futuristic, or science fiction novels)?

8. Using Point of View

    Can you effectively maintain a single point of view for an extended passage? Have you intentionally given the dog, the cat, and the rocking chair a point of view? Do you have a preference (or an obsession) with writing from single versus multiple points of view?

9. Ending Chapters

    Do you know when to end a chapter? Does your ending include an element of surprise or misunderstanding or mystery that will encourage a reader to turn the page (rather than put down the book)? Do you use subplots to delay the reader's gratification of expectation?

10. Revision

    Do you write a first draft with revision in mind? Do you see revision as a positive part of the writing process? Do you have the ability to look objectively and critically at your own work? Are you willing to throw away large sections of your work in the revision process?

11. Editing
    Does the time-consuming, detailed process of "finish work" give you great satisfaction? Is grammar prominent in your repertoire of writer's skills? Can you punctuate effectively?

12. Doing Research
    Do you have a good sense of balance regarding the mix of fact and fiction? Do you have the discipline to set a deadline on the amount of research in your preparation to write? Do you have a good network and understanding of available resources?

13. Writing Habits…Discipline
    Are you a goal setter? Are you driven to achieve those goals? Do you need positive incentives to motivate you?

14. Taking Criticism
    Do you refuse to pout, sulk, or kick the dog because of something your critique partner pointed out about your work? Can you separate yourself from your work and take a positive approach to criticism that is being offered objectively? Can you separate the person (the critique partner) from the comments and forgive them some time in the next century? Do you revel in retaliation?

15. The Business of Writing
    Are you able to put as much energy into the business aspects of your work as you do on the creative aspects? Are you confident in your knowledge and skills in both areas? Can you (once again) separate yourself from your creative efforts and see your writing as a "product"?

You've finished the quiz! What you do next should fall under one of the following categories:

- Never mind burying the thing…bake the chicken.

- Take classes, read, and try to develop your areas of weakness.

- Borrow or buy a copy of *Marriage of Minds: Collaborative Fiction Writing* by Nikoo & Jim McGoldrick, and then consider collaborating with someone who complements your strengths and weaknesses.

The Order of Things

or

Structuring the Synopsis

As writers who have dreams of selling our work, we all occasionally need to craft a synopsis.

Many books and articles have been written that expound on the appropriate style and content needed to produce the successful synopsis—we're not going to repeat any of that. If you're online, then you know that you can find the guidelines for submission for nearly all publishers with the click of your mouse—we're not going there, either. We have only two suggestions that we want to pass on. For us, they are the only two laws of synopsis writing that we live by:

1. Remember that the synopsis is a *selling* tool.

2. Define your story in a way that shows the potential agent/editor that you know how to *structure* your story.

The first point is fairly self-explanatory, so we won't belabor it. As we write the synopsis, though, we can easily get wrapped up in trying to include all of the points that the reference articles and books said we need to have in our synopsis, and in so doing, lose track of what the synopsis will be used for.

So let's back up a step. After the cover letter, an editor/agent will probably read the chapters you've submitted—or at least the beginning of those chapters. If the writing doesn't grab them, they will probably just move it to the "Rejection" pile. After all, the potential agent or editor is looking for a saleable product. In other words, they are "reading to reject," all the while hoping that the quality story will emerge and engage them immediately. If the chapters keep their attention and enthusiasm, they will then turn to the synopsis.

Let's assume that your prose makes Charlotte Bronte look like a rank amateur and your creativity with character would make Charles Dickens drool with envy. On top of all that, the story you've thought up is an absolute winner. Then what must the synopsis do? It must be written in a way that an editor can take it into a meeting for the purpose of "selling" you and your work to her peers and superiors—people in both production and marketing.

So how do you best present your story (and yourself as writer) in your synopsis? Show them that you have a story that has been crafted with a definable structure…even if you haven't finished the book and have absolutely no clue how you are going to tie all the loose ends together at the end. And here's how…

Engage the potential agent/editor/marketing manager immediately with a highly charged opening. It can be a "high concept" description of the work, or a high-energy encapsulation of the opening.

Next, quickly give a sense of who the central characters really are, what draws them together, and what they will have to overcome (internally and externally) in order to succeed and still get together in the end.

Now comes the tricky part—showing structure. Incidentally, in a longer, more detailed synopsis, we actually separate the text into segments that we label, "The Players," "The Back Story," "The Story."

In "The Back Story" section of the synopsis, we give the relevant information that the agent/editor needs to know and to understand the story. It is material that we would gradually feed into the book later on, since we like to start our novels in the middle of some action.

When we've given just the essential info, though, we break off and use a phrase like "The novel begins with…" or "The first act of our story begins with…"

In this first part, we will present the early plot action that pushes our major characters into the conflict that drives the story. Along with the main characters and the setting, we present at this point in the synopsis exactly what the main question is in the story—or rather what might keep the characters from achieving their individual goals in the action of the story.

Once we've conveyed that, we use a term like "Act Two of the novel occurs when the action shifts from…." In this section of the synopsis, we try to show that we have a series of events that will present the characters with obstacles that they must overcome. Meeting and sometimes failing the tests these obstacles present are much of what stories are made of.

In the synopsis, we want to show that the main characters each have a role in forging the outcome of the story, working together (or against each other), and developing as a result of their actions. Usually, when the development of relationship between the hero and heroine has reached the point where they can resolve the main question that was presented in the first part of the story, we need to throw another serious barrier in their way. Linda Seger calls this "raising the stakes," in her book *Making a Good Script Great*. This is where the story moves into Act Three of the action.

Act Three is usually the shortest of the three section of the synopsis. It consists of speeded up action culminating in the climax, where the main question or problem is finally resolved. Here, also, the future is secured for the hero's and heroine's newly formed relationship. Here, we say things like "X-action launches us toward the exciting conclusion where…" and later, "In a climatic scene…" How specific you are in this section is dependent on whether your story is done or not. If, however, you have given the potential agent/editor a sense that you can successfully and logically get your characters to the climax, then the details of the conclusion are fairly secondary in importance.

We believe that this structure exists in nearly all stories—we present the characters and the main question; we present the actions and events in which our characters develop; and then we put them in a situation where they succeed or they fail, thereby resolving the main question.

Crafting your synopsis in this way shows a potential buyer that your know how to craft a story. It says that there will be no "sagging middle" because there is a series of events that will keep the action moving forward. It says that there will be a satisfactory conclusion because we consciously presented a question in the opening that will be answered at the climax.

It says…here is a story you can sell.

A Restless Muse

Gypsies. That's us. Gypsies.

Of course, we say that without any thought as to whether the term is politically correct at the moment. But that is what we are. Have been for ever. Sure, for as long as we can remember, we wanted to be writers. Actually, it was before that. In our cribs, we knew we wanted to be writers. Even in utero, we were each composing. Nikoo was keeping a journal. Jim was writing poetry and complaining about the poor lighting. But we digress.

Truth is, long before we knew or cared about what we wanted to be in life, we were gypsies. We moved fifty-five times in the first five years of our marriage…and that wasn't because we had to. We just felt like it. Between the two of us, we've had about five hundred fifty-five different careers. Not jobs…*careers*. Okay, maybe not that many.

That was us…restless, fearless, reckless, penniless. Note that "less" is the connecting link between our descriptors. But you get the picture. We've always been footloose risk-takers. From our point of view, these are very positive qualities. From our family and friends' points of view…well, not so good. Honestly, we were never very good at following our loved ones advice. We just have always figured that this is our life, and we've never felt we needed an opinion poll to live it.

Oh, yes, this article is about writing, isn't it…

Individually, we each have been writing for all our lives. And yes, Jim is still complaining about the poor lighting. Somehow, though, we've been collaborating for fifteen years and penned twenty-seven books. So how do two restless souls like us function in the world of genre fiction, where the fans are loyal to the authors they love and editors more than nudge their writers into a niche the publishing house can be comfortable with? For some writers, it can be something like *How Stella Got Her Groove Back: the Dark Side*.

We're getting ahead of ourselves. Our first literary persona, May McGoldrick, was born during the heady weeks following the sale of our first book to NAL. Or was it Signet? No, it was Penguin. Which was *before* it became Penguin Putnam. Right, and the name of the imprint was Topaz, the Jewel of Historical Romance. We were as happy as a couple of clams at high tide. On top of our world. Of course, clams live in a world of shifting sands. Which really didn't bother us. We are, don't forget, gypsies. One thing we didn't know was that our restless spirit was infectious. Even our soon to be bought out publishing house was not exempt. Nor was the editorial staff. For our first four books, we had four different editors.

They said we weren't the reason for them moving on, but there were *four* of them… Despite those beach chairs that kept disappearing from our sandy shore, we kept on writing. (Jeez, we're starting to mix metaphors, aren't we?)

A few years…and nine books…later, our restlessness kicked in again. We wanted to write something else. We had different stories in us. New worlds to explore. We used the excuse that we could write faster than our publisher could put us on the shelves. So we started writing a blitz of proposals. Nonfiction, young adult, paranormal, suspense…and anything else that tickled our imagination that week. The confidence of selling that first book years earlier gave us the encouragement we needed. We were certain that what we'd learned in one genre could transfer to other settings, different characters, other time periods. We were storytellers at heart. It was research that set these different stories apart. And with a Ph.D. partner in the house, research was our middle name.

Shock of shocks…there were rejections. Lots of them. (You should read our "A-Z of Rejection" article.) And there were other setbacks, too. But we had donned our leather skins. We were facing rough terrain, but we would pass over it. We were pursuing a career that we loved. What else could one ask for? Well, actually, a truck full of money would have been nice.

That blitz of proposals ended up opening a few doors. We wrote romantic suspense for Mira, a book of nonfiction for Heinemann, a young adult novel for Avon/HarperCollins, and more historical romance for NAL.

We kept writing, but the old restlessness kept kicking in again every couple of years. We switched from historical to contemporary for our second young adult novel, *Tropical Kiss*, which is set in Aruba. Then, we decided to do a historical romantic comedy that was essentially a parody of *Arsenic and Old Lace*. That's how Nicole Cody and *Love and Mayhem* came about.

Even our romantic suspense novels found stronger elements of techno-thriller edging in. With an engineer in the house, we had to get more technical, and with each story, we had something new to share with the reader. *Five in a Row* involved the technology called "drive-by-wire," which is a system that is involved in the design of all new cars. Readers were pretty surprised to learn that a computer ran their family automobile. They were even more surprised to know that someone could possibly hack into that computer! *New York Times* printed an article, "Can a Virus Hitch a Ride on Your Car," after our book came out. Their list of experts for the article included people that we used researching *Five in a Row.*

Silent Waters dealt with the hijacking of a nuclear submarine. Between the two of us, we had fifteen years of submarine construction experience, so it was great fun to share some of that knowledge.

The Project dealt with nano-technology and a mother caught up in a rash of school shootings. *The Deadliest Strain*, which won the Connecticut Press Club's Best Fiction Award, deals with the life of a Kurdish women going back home after spending five years in a ghost prison in Afghanistan. And in 2009, the two releases, *The Puppet Master* and *Blind Eye* were edge-of-your-seat suspense thrillers that kept readers turning the pages.

The bottom line is, other than leaving a trail of pen names behind, we've found the profession that offers a sense of excitement that soothes our restless souls. Since starting to write, we've only moved once. That says something. So much for the gypsy life. We're looking and acting almost like responsible adults. Almost. Our sons have even started calling us boring. And that's a compliment, considering our checkered past.

Besides, somebody once wrote, "My life is boring…but my fiction is exciting."

We'll take that…for now.

How to Keep Working While the World Parties Around You

Actually, we think Gustav Flaubert said, "My life is dull so that my fiction is not."

We've been writing together for over fifteen years now. In that time we've produced twenty-seven novels that have seen the murky light of the bookstore. We've won awards and become friends with readers and other writers and given workshops and talks at conferences. We've also seen our two boys grow into fine young men. Somehow.

And we also have neighbors who think we must constantly be away, because they never see us. Jetsetters that they think we are, we are asked if we've been away on some research trip to an exotic place or on some worldwide book tour or even, "Were you guys just on *Regis and Kelly*?"

The truth is that—like most of those who also labor in the trenches of commercial fiction—we are usually at our computers. Day in, day out, we scratch for every minute we can get to meet our deadlines and to produce the story proposal that will throw our editors into such fits of delirium that we will be vaulted into the ethereal realms of literary stardom. In short, we are working our butts off to pay the mortgage.

And yet, how do we do that—keep our word count up—while the world around us seems to be having a party?

To begin, we need to remember that we are not alone in this struggle. Writers have dealt with this problem for ages, and some were more successful at dealing with it than others. F. Scott Fitzgerald, for example, was not very good at it. If there was even a chance of a party in any given tri-state area, he was there. The only time he seemed to be able to write was when he and Zelda were miserable. There was a point, however, when it occurred to him that he might be able to live more cheaply abroad (where he knew fewer people to party with) and he could work with less interruption (because he knew fewer people to party with). Unfortunately, Paris and the Riviera turned out to BE parties.

Others had mixed success. John Steinbeck, it's rumored, believed that the author should not have sex while writing. We don't think he meant no sex while *typing*, but rather no sex during a period of literary creativity. In any event, this monastic approach cost him a marriage, by all accounts.

Virginia Woolf, in writing about the difficulty of being a woman and a writer, concluded that those who wish to write need to have a "room of one's own." The "isolation=production" theory.

Hemingway—who by the way thought Steinbeck's position sheer madness and had at least twenty-five or thirty successful marriages—bought into Woolf's idea. At his Key West home, he had a study that could only be accessed by way of a catwalk from the second floor of his house.

Charles Dickens was another. On his estate, he had a little Swiss chalet built with a entry ladder that he could pull up while he was working. There is also the story of a contemporary American writer (who will remain nameless for fear of lawsuits) who stayed home to write and care for his toddler while his wife went off to earn their living. He pushed the child's playpen in front of the TV, put a piece of plywood over the top, and went to his study to work. He said he knew he would feel guilty about it in later life, but he simply *had* to write. Incidentally, Hemingway also sent his kids to boarding school.

As for us, we are constantly struggling with this problem. We are certainly not advocates of the Steinbeck method. We were also unwilling to lock our kids away so that we could write. As a result, we've had to work on our scheduling.

Yes, scheduling is the key. For us, summer has always been a horrible time for writing. School vacation, family visits, grass needs cutting, the garden needs weeding, the body (ours and the dog's) needs walking, the beach (less than an hour away) needs visiting, strawberries (and raspberries and blueberries) need picking. And canning. You get the picture. And then there is golf. Summers are bad for writing. So we try, usually without success, to schedule our personal deadlines before the summer starts, even if the editor says September 1st is really the due date.

When we're forced to work in the summer (which is really always), we try to take advantage of rainy days. We try to get a 6 AM start (while the boys, often including Jim, are still asleep), or we simply work the 8-midnight shift…a lot.

As we all know, working while raising children is tough. We've all heard the line about, "Unless there's smoke, blood, or bone showing, don't interrupt me while I'm writing." Since we're essentially nervous parents, that's never worked for us. One thing we've found sometimes works is the "reciprocation=isolation" technique. This means that if you have twenty kids over to your house for a play day, then you should get at least ten invitations from responsible fellow moms for play days. That means ten days when your children will be out of the house and somewhere reasonably safe. Lose a workday, but gain ten. Actually, this works more in theory than in practice, but it's always worth a shot. We think it's far better than dropping them off at the mall.

To get our writing time in while the world continues to spin, however, a number of things have had to be sacrificed. Our children have never been on the casualty list, but TV was first to take the hit. As a result, we never saw *Seinfeld*…or *Friends*…or *Frasier*. We *might* know Oprah if we saw her in the grocery store, but we wouldn't know Kelly Ripa if she showed up at our door with her entire camera crew, we're sorry to say. We occasionally watch movies, but we've found that getting our movies from NetFlix works better for us than Blockbuster because we can keep a movie for months if we're pressed to write and we can't find the time to watch it.

Sleep is another thing that has suffered for our craft. Sometimes, nighttime is the only time to get it done.

Other than that, we find that we've developed an odd (sort of masochistic) reward system for ourselves. We set up achievable daily word count goals that will get our manuscript done before the due date, then we "reward" ourselves for making the day's goal. For example, if we make the word count by 4 PM, Jim gets to mow the lawn. If we make it by 8 PM, Nikoo gets to weed the garden. Ironing. Garage cleaning. Going to the post office. Answering email. And on and on. Really fun things!

Our life is dull so that our fiction is not. Well, we hope that's true.

Finally, we use Advanced Visualization Techniques to help us write while the world is partying around us. We've heard Nora Roberts say that she visualizes her fifth grade nun, Sister Mary Something-or-Other, standing over her with her metal ruler in hand saying, "Work, Nora, work. Idle hands, you know…"

What works best for us is occasionally closing our eyes and visualizing our lives without writing. There we are, with plenty of time on our hands to do all kinds of fun, leisure activities. Yes, we can see ourselves. We're fit and carefree. The sun is warm on our faces.

'This is the life!' we tell each other…as we push our possessions along in our battered grocery cart.

Yes, indeed. Visualization=Motivation.

Changing Gears: Writing Suspense vs. Historicals

May McGoldrick, a historical romance writer, is a diligent and industrious professional. Jan Coffey is a bit neurotic, frankly.

But with good reason. Jan writes contemporary suspense thrillers.

To be honest, May and Jan are really both the same people. We (Nikoo and Jim) have been collaborating as May McGoldrick on historicals and Jan Coffey for thrillers for a number of years. Interestingly enough, we're finding that there are differences in writing stories in the two genres.

First of all, we should tell you that we started setting our early stories in the 16th century period because we had some academic background in the time period. Write what you know, they told us.

But in writing historical novels as May McGoldrick, we've always tried, as well, to create new stories, new characters, and new problems for our heroines and heroes to overcome. To do that, we've pushed ourselves to stretch into areas where we have needed to learn new things. We have to admit that if we *only* wrote about what we knew, we never would have written about murderous lairds, or covens of Highland women, or cross-dressing artists, or children with physical handicaps, or promiscuous English queens!

Those things are just not a part of everyday life in the McGoldrick household.

At least, not the way we understand Jan Coffey's world of murder and mayhem and bottom-dwelling criminal types. Our years in the shipyards of New England were not spent in vain. No, the 'suspense' isn't the problem. The 'contemporary' part is. You see, Jim has just barely joined the 1990's, never mind the 21st century.

The solution for us is, of course, research and imagination. The only difference between the act of writing historicals and writing contemporary thrillers is mindset (okay, and language…and plotting, too…and setting…and a few other things that we will get to in this article…).

In moving from the mindset of the historical writer to the mindset of the suspense writer, we stop reading *Britain* magazine. We hold off planning trips to places with castles and talking over breakfast about the portrayal of executions in *Braveheart*.

Instead, we immerse ourselves in the contemporary world. Now, we go out for breakfast at local diners. We hang out in airports to watch people go through security checkpoints. We read newspapers and great contemporary suspense novels and watch *CSI*.

For us, there is a vague line between mindset and research. Perhaps the word 'research' connotes the finding of specific details, but for us, research is a seductively pleasurable pastime that takes us, mind and soul, out of our daily life—and away from the writing we should be accomplishing for that day. It places us smack dab in the world that we are researching.

But there is a difference here, too. When we are May McGoldrick, writing historicals set (for example) in 1760's England, we read things like James Boswell's *London Journal of 1762-1763*. When we are Jan Coffey, writing a thriller set amid the mansions of Newport or shipyards in Groton we read *Town & Country* and *Popular Mechanics*.

As May, we study about the wool industry of the 1500's and watch the History Channel (Actually, though, it doesn't have to be the History Channel. Any show with ruins will do.) As Jan, we watch *COPS* and study the police reports of the *Philadelphia Inquirer* and *New York Times*. Our research of the contemporary world includes finding out the meaning of the latest teenage slang, whether spoken or written during Instant Messenger chats or on Facebook (Yes, we now know what terms such as G2G, TTYL, U, UR, and BRB mean. <g>).

In planning and plotting out our stories, we find there are differences, too. As May, we find that we do about 20% of our planning up front and 80% of it as we write.

As Jan we do 80% of our plotting up front, and only 20% of it in the process of actually writing the book. In writing suspense, we're still open to the changes that present themselves as we write, but we try to think ahead as much as we can.

Maybe because of the difference in the pre-writing stage, even the synopses we send to our editors are different. May McGoldrick's synopsis for her historicals is shorter and more character-oriented, while Jan Coffey's synopsis is longer and far more detailed, particularly in the description of the action.

But how about the actual writing? How do we change gears there? That is a tough question, because our physical process is still the same. Nikoo still writes most of the first draft, with Jim chirping in constantly and at the most inopportune moments. At the same time, he is five or ten pages behind her (or sometimes thirty or forty), madly revising and adding and deleting. Luckily, Nikoo carefully changes the text back to the way it should be later.

But there are some differences. In May's stories, the writing tries to capture some of the texture of the historical period. As a result, her scenes are sometimes longer than those of her contemporary counterpart, who finds that short scenes keep the pace of a story rocketing along. In Jan's stories, the writing tries to capture, as well, the contemporary attitude of her characters through their dialogue.

In revision, we find that we need to shift our gears a little, too. As May McGoldrick, we live by the *Webster's Ninth Collegiate Dictionary* and the *Oxford English Dictionary* and their references to the dates that words came into use. As Jan Coffey, we can use terms and put things into our suspense novels that we can't in our historicals. For example, what a treat it is to be able to say that a character was "mesmerized" by another character. Since F.A. Mesmer, the early hypnotist, was not even alive until the 18th century, it just won't do to use the term in the 1500's.

There are frightening differences between historicals vs. contemporaries, too. Because of the larger number of characters, and because she likes to end her chapters at 'cliffhanger' points in the narrative, Jan finds that she has a lot more plot threads that she needs to keep track of. Yes, all those unanswered questions that arise in the course of the story must be answered before the last page. Jan has far more of them to worry about than May does.

Even in shipping the book, May McGoldrick and Jan Coffey work differently. May finishes her historical and ships it off with a month to spare. Jan finds Nikoo and Jim prying the suspense novel out of each other's fingers at the last minute on the deadline date and chasing the UPS guy down the street.

And it doesn't end there, either. May finds that she can relax in the aftermath of sending off the historical. Jan is lying awake at night, trying to remember what loose thread she left open in her suspense novel.

Of course, then it starts all over again…happily.

Which brings us back to mindset. But if you hear that neurotic old Jan Coffey has bumped off May McGoldrick in her sleep some night, just don't be surprised.

The A-Z of Rejection

This is just a sampling of our Rejection Portfolio, compiled while writing alone and as partners. The English professor in Jim requires the portfolio; the engineer in Nikoo requires the list…

A…not Appropriate for our list. Good luck placing your work elsewhere!

B…Dear Bob, (Wait a minute! Who's Bob?)…We're sorry to say your science fiction novel is not right for our list. Good luck in placing your work elsewhere!

C…after Careful consideration, we regret to say that your manuscript is not right for our list. Good luck in placing your work elsewhere!

D…looking for more Down-to-earth novels. Good luck in placing your work elsewhere!

E…I'm afraid I lack the Enthusiasm you have every right to expect in your agent. Good luck in placing your work elsewhere!

F…we do not Feel this is suitable for our list. Good luck in placing your work elsewhere!

G…society rich Glamour doesn't work for us. Good luck in placing your work elsewhere!

H…Historical romances are no longer selling. Good luck in placing your work elsewhere!

I…Interesting proposal, but I'm afraid it doesn't meet the needs of our list at this time. Good luck in placing your work elsewhere!

J…Jim who? I didn't go to kindergarten with any Jim McGoldrick. But good luck in placing your work elsewhere!

K…not the Kind of project that we feel we could be successful with. Good luck in placing your work elsewhere!

L…Lithuanian mysteries are no longer selling. Good luck in placing your work elsewhere!

M…Marianne X, the editor you queried in 1964, has retired. The cleaning staff, finding your manuscript, has decided that your work doesn't meet the needs of our present list. Good luck in placing your work elsewhere!

N…Not sufficiently compelled by your work to make an offer of publication. Good luck in placing your work elsewhere!

O…Octogenarian romances are no longer selling. Good luck in placing your work elsewhere!

P…Paranormal elements are not appropriate for our lists. Good luck in placing your work elsewhere!

Q…we receive Quite a large volume of manuscripts. This same volume prevents us from replying with individual comments. Good luck in placing your work elsewhere!

R…Regret the seemingly impersonal nature of this letter… (Not signed, but stamped.) Good luck in placing your work elsewhere!

S…Sorry to tell you that your proposed manuscript doesn't seem right for our list. (Not signed, and not stamped) Good luck in placing your work elsewhere!

T…The editor you queried just threw himself off the fifteenth floor ledge. His note said your work was not right for our list at this time. Good luck in placing your work elsewhere!

U…Unsolicited submissions are not being accepted at this time. Good luck in placing your work elsewhere!

V…taking on Very few new projects, and this just doesn't seem right for me. Good luck in placing your work elsewhere!

W…We love you dearly, but if you think you are moving back home now that you are unemployed writers, think again. Good luck in placing your work somewhere!

X…eXcept for the weak characterization, overly complicated plot, suffocating amounts of description and detail, and serious punctuation errors, your proposal almost swept us away. Good luck in placing your work elsewhere!

Y…You will never place this with a bona fide publishing house in a trillion years. Good luck in placing your work elsewhere!

Z…a Zillion dollars wouldn't be enough for such a work as this. Sorry, we can't afford you. Good luck in placing your work elsewhere!

Still licking their wounds after fifteen years of rejections, Jim and Nikoo have learned that perseverance pays off.

The A-Z of Writing

Anyone who says he wants to be a writer and isn't writing, doesn't. *Ernest Hemingway*

Books aren't written, they're rewritten. *Michael Crichton*

Critics are like eunuchs in a harem: they know how it's done, they've seen it done every day, but they are unable to do it themselves. *Brendan Behan*

Don't get it right, get it written. *James Thurber (to a group of aspiring journalists)*

Emotions move a reader through a story. *Ann Copeland*

First, we breathe life in our characters. Second, we watch them develop. Third, we listen when they speak to us. Then, we get professional help.
Aristotle Micklefuss (a close personal friend of the McGoldricks)

Good writing requires good rhythms and good words. *Richard Marius*

How do I know what I think until I see what I say? *E. M. Forster*

I write, therefore I am. *Samuel Johnson*

Just write a good sentence—that's the postulate I go by. *Richard Ford*

Knowledge of what you love somehow comes to you; you don't have to read nor analyze nor study.
Jessamyn West (to her parents after flunking out of her nineteenth grad school)

Love is the spirit that motivates the artist's journey. *Eric Maisel*

Meaning is in small things. *Marvin Bell (Tinker's little brother)*

No pessimist ever discovered the secrets of the stars, or sailed to an uncharted land, or opened a new heaven to the human spirit. *Helen Keller*

One line of dialogue is worth paragraphs of description. No matter what you say about a character, if he doesn't speak, he hasn't truly come alive. *Leslie Epstein*

Professionals constantly search for ways to grow.
Nikoo and Jim McGoldrick (upon learning that both of their children wanted to go to graduate school)

Query letters work best when addressed to live editors.
Boccaccio (to a writing class during the Black Plague)

Read over your compositions and, when you meet a passage which you think is particularly fine, strike it out. *Samuel Johnson*

Style is a matter of vision, not technique. *Marcel Proust*

Talent is cheap. What matters is discipline. *Andre Dubus*

Until you make peace with who you are, you'll never be content with what you have.
Doris Mortman

Virtually every page is a cliffhanger—you've got to force them to turn it. *Dr. Seuss*

Write what makes you happy. *O. Henry*

X marks the spot. *R. L. Stevenson (We couldn't find an X! So…sue us.)*

You only live once—but if you work it right, once is enough. *Joe E. Lewis*

Zinfandel is a cheap substitute when a writer really needs a friend…but it is cheap.
Ernest and Julie O'Gallo

When they are not misquoting Bartlett and company, Jim and Nikoo McGoldrick write fiction for living.

REFERENCES & RESOURCES

Icebreakers:

http://www.topten.org/content/tt.AU20.htm

http://www.funattic.com/game_icebreaker.htm

http://www.firststepstraining.com/resources/activities/archive/activity_large_ice.htm

http://www.hu.mtu.edu/~klwest/troupe/games/improv/human.html

http://www.icebreakers.ws/team-building

http://wilderdom.com/games/Icebreakers.html

http://honolulu.hawaii.edu/intranet/committees/FacDevCom/guidebk/teachtip/breakice.htm

http://www.residentassistant.com/games/

Survival scenario exercises promoting communication and collaboration.

http://wilderdom.com/games/descriptions/SurvivalScenarios.html

Poetry

http://www.youngpoets.ca/english/teaching_form_poetry_part_two

http://www.docstoc.com/docs/4979748/example-of-a-couplet-poem

Other Sources referred to in this book:

Cameron, Julia. *The Artist's Way: A Spiritual Path to Higher Creativity.* New York:
  Putnam, 1992.

Druker, Phil. University of Idaho.
  http://www.class.uidaho.edu/druker/nonfic.html

Goleman, Daniel. *The Creative Spirit: Companion to the PBS Television Series.* New
  York; Penguin, 1992.

Larsen, Michael. *How to Write a Book Proposal.* New York: Writers Digest Books, 2004.

Levine, Mel. *A Mind at A Time: America's Top Learning Expert Shows How Every Child Can Succeed.* New York; Simon & Schuster, 2002.

Lounsberry, Barbara. "Guidelines for Writing Creative NonFiction." *The Literature of Reality,* G. Talese & B. Lounsberry, eds. New York: HarperCollins, 1996.

Malkin, Michael. *Training the Young Actor.* London; Magdalen House, 1981.

McGoldrick, James A. & Nikoo K. *Marriage of Minds: Collaborative Fiction Writing.* Portsmouth; Heinemann, 2000.

Seger, Linda. *Making a Good Script Great.* Hollywood; Samuel French, 1994.

Wagner, Tony. *The Global Achievement Gap: Why Even Our Best Schools Don't Teach The New Survival Skills Our Children Need—and What We Can Do About It.* New York; Basic Books, 2008.

AUTHOR'S NOTE

We hope you have found this book helpful.

We have vast experience in many aspects of writing, publication, and teaching. Each year, we conduct a number of seminars on topics of collaboration and creativity for all age groups. We also give "fiction-specific" workshops on the subjects of novel writing and publication.

We are available for Classroom and Educator workshops and also for school visits. You can contact us at:

Nikoo & Jim McGoldrick
P.O. Box 665
Watertown, CT 06795

JanCoffey@JanCoffey.com

www.JanCoffey.com

Additional copies of this book and all of our other works in print can be purchased through our website, or they can be ordered through any bookseller across the country.

Thank you.

Step Write Up

"LEARNING AND INNOVATION SKILLS"

"Learning and innovation skills increasingly are being recognized as those that separate students who are prepared for a more and more complex life and work environments in the 21st century, and those who are not. A focus on creativity, critical thinking, communication and collaboration is essential to prepare students for the future."

—*Partnership for 21st Century Skills*

Complete Book List as of 2009

Writing Nonfiction as James and Nikoo McGoldrick

Marriage of Minds: Collaborative Fiction Writing

Writing fiction as Jan Coffey:

Blind Eye
The Puppet Master
The Deadliest Strain
The Project
Silent Waters
Five in a Row
Tropical Kiss (Young Adult Novel)
Fourth Victim
Triple Threat
Twice Burned
Trust Me Once

Writing Fiction as May McGoldrick:

Dreams of Destiny
Captured Dreams
Borrowed Dreams
The Rebel
Tess and The Highlander (Young Adult Novel)
The Promise
The Firebrand
The Enchantress
The Dreamer
Flame
The Intended
Beauty of The Mist
Heart of Gold
Angel of Skye
Thistle and The Rose

Writing Fiction as Nicole Cody:

Love and Mayhem